WORLD
HISTORY SERIES ■■■

The Lewis and Clark Expedition

Titles in the World History Series

The
Lewis and Clark
Expedition

by
Eleanor J. Hall

Lucent Books, P.O. Box 289011, San Diego, CA 92198-9011

Library of Congress Cataloging-in-Publication Data

Hall, Eleanor J.
    The Lewis and Clark expedition / by Eleanor J. Hall.
        p. cm.—(World history series)
    Includes bibliographical references and index.
    ISBN 1-56006-291-6 (Lib. Ed. : alk. paper)
    1. Lewis and Clark Expedition (1804–1806)—Juvenile liter-
ature. 2. Lewis, Meriwether, 1774–1809—Juvenile literature.
3. Clark, William, 1770–1838—Juvenile literature. I.Title.
II. Series.
F592.7.H24   1996
917.804'2—dc20   95-11708
[B]   CIP
                                                              AC

Copyright 1996 by Lucent Books, Inc., P.O. Box 289011,
San Diego, California, 92198-9011

Printed in the U.S.A.

Contents

Foreword

Each year on the first day of school, nearly every history teacher faces the task of explaining why his or her students should study history. One logical answer to this question is that exploring what happened in our past explains how the things we often take for granted—our customs, ideas, and institutions—came to be. As statesman and historian Winston Churchill put it, "Every nation or group of nations has its own tale to tell. Knowledge of the trials and struggles is necessary to all who would comprehend the problems, perils, challenges, and opportunities which confront us today." Thus, a study of history puts modern ideas and institutions in perspective. For example, though the founders of the United States were talented and creative thinkers, they clearly did not invent the concept of democracy. Instead, they adapted some democratic ideas that had originated in ancient Greece and with which the Romans, the British, and others had experimented. An exploration of these cultures, then, reveals their very real connection to us through institutions that continue to shape our daily lives.

Another reason often given for studying history is the idea that lessons exist in the past from which contemporary societies can benefit and learn. This idea, although controversial, has always been an intriguing one for historians. Those that agree that society can benefit from the past often quote philosopher George Santayana's famous statement, "Those who cannot remember the past are condemned to repeat it." Historians who ascribe to Santayana's philosophy believe that, for example, studying the events that led up to the major world wars or other significant historical events would allow society to chart a different and more favorable course in the future.

Just as difficult as convincing students to realize the importance of studying history is the search for useful and interesting supplementary materials that present historical events in a context that can be easily understood. The volumes in Lucent Books' World History Series attempt to present a broad, balanced, and penetrating view of the march of history. Ancient Egypt's important wars and rulers, for example, are presented against the rich and colorful backdrop of Egyptian religious, social, and cultural developments. The series engages the reader by enhancing historical events with these cultural contexts. For example, in *Ancient Greece*, the text covers the role of women in that society. Slavery is discussed in *The Roman Empire*, as well as how slaves earned their freedom. The numerous and varied aspects of everyday life in these and other societies are explored in each volume of the series. Additionally, the series covers the major political, cultural, and philosophical ideas as the torch of civilization is passed from ancient Mesopotamia and Egypt, through Greece, Rome, Medieval Europe, and other world cultures, to the modern day.

The material in the series is formatted in a thorough, precise, and organized manner. Each volume offers the reader a comprehensive and clearly written overview of an important historical event or period. The topic under discussion is placed in a broad historical context. For example, *The Italian Renaissance* begins with a discussion of the High Middle Ages and the loss of central control that allowed certain Italian cities to develop artistically. The book ends by looking forward to the Reformation and interpreting the societal changes that grew out of the Renaissance. Thus, students are not only involved in an historical era, but also enveloped by the events leading up to that era and the events following it.

One important and unique feature in the World History Series is the primary and secondary source quotations that richly supplement each volume. These quotes are useful in a number of ways. First, they allow students access to sources they would not normally be exposed to because of the difficulty and obscurity of the original source. The quotations range from interesting anecdotes to far-sighted cultural perspectives and are drawn from historical witnesses both past and present. Second, the quotes demonstrate how and where historians themselves derive their information on the past as they strive to reach a consensus on historical events. Lastly, all of the quotes are footnoted, familiarizing students with the citation process and allowing them to verify quotes and/or look up the original source if the quote piques their interest.

Finally, the books in the World History Series provide a detailed launching point for further research. Each book contains a bibliography specifically geared toward student research. A second, annotated bibliography introduces students to all the sources the author consulted when compiling the book. A chronology of important dates gives students an overview, at a glance, of the topic covered. Where applicable, a glossary of terms is included.

In short, the series is designed not only to acquaint readers with the basics of history, but also to make them aware that their lives are a part of an ongoing human saga. Perhaps they will then come to the same realization as famed historian Arnold Toynbee. In his monumental work, *A Study of History*, he wrote about becoming aware of history flowing through him in a mighty current, and of his own life "welling like a wave in the flow of this vast tide."

Important Dates in the History of the Lewis and Clark Expedition

1801	1802	1803	1804	1805	18

1801

February
President-elect Thomas Jefferson selects Meriwether Lewis as his secretary

March
Jefferson takes office as third president of the United States

1803

January 18
Jefferson sends secret message to Congress asking approval for an expedition

May 2
Louisiana Purchase is signed in Paris (dated April 30)

June 19
Lewis asks Clark to accompany him on the expedition

June 20
Jefferson sends instructions to Lewis for the expedition

July 18
Clark accepts Lewis's offer to accompany him on the expedition

August 31
Lewis leaves Pittsburgh in a new keelboat bound for St. Louis

October
Clark joins Lewis in Indiana Territory

October 19
Senate ratifies Louisiana Purchase

December
Lewis and Clark reach St. Louis and begin encampment at nearby Camp Wood

December 20
United States takes possession of Lower Louisiana at New Orleans

1804

March 10
United States takes possession of Upper Louisiana at St. Louis; Lewis is official representative at ceremonies

May 14
Expedition leaves Camp Wood

August 3
Captains hold council with Missouri and Oto Indians at Council Bluffs

August 18
Deserter Moses Reed is court-martialed

August 20
Sergeant Floyd dies

September 25
Expedition has confrontation with Teton Sioux

October
Expedition arrives at Mandan villages (in present-day North Dakota)

1805

February 11
Baby boy is born to Sacagawea and Charbonneau

April 7
Expedition leaves the Mandans; keelboat is sent back to St. Louis

June 22–July 15
Portage around Great Falls of the Missouri River

July 27–29
Camp at Three Forks (in present-day Montana)

August 13
Lewis makes contact with the Shoshone at continental divide (Lemhi Pass)

August 17
Sacagawea is reunited with her people

August 30
Expedition leaves Shoshone village

September
Expedition crosses Bitterroot Mountains; makes camp with Nez Percé

October 7
Expedition's canoes are launched on the Clearwater River (in present-day Idaho)

October 16
Expedition reaches the Columbia River

November 14
Lewis and a few others first reach the Pacific Ocean

December 30
Winter camp at Fort Clatsop in Oregon Territory is completed

1806

March 23
Expedition leaves Fort Clatsop, heading homeward

May
Expedition establishes camp near Nez Percé villages while snow melts in Bitterroot Mountains

June 24-30
Expedition crosses Bitterroots on the way home

July 3
At Traveller's Rest, two parties are formed for river explorations

July 14–August 3
Clark and party explore the Yellowstone River

July 17–28
Lewis and party explore Maria's River

July 27
Lewis and party kill two Blackfoot Indians in skirmish

August
The divided party is reunited, returns to the Mandan villages, and departs for Washington, accompanied by a Mandan chief and his family

September 23
Expedition arrives at St. Louis

Later Years

1807
Lewis is appointed governor of Upper Louisiana Territory

March 1807
Clark is appointed brigadier general of militia for Upper Louisiana Territory and superintendent of Indian affairs at St. Louis

1809
Lewis dies

1812
Sacagawea dies

1838
Clark dies

An Idea Becomes Reality

Almost two hundred years have passed since two young army captains, Meriwether Lewis and William Clark, led a small band of soldiers, civilians, and one Indian woman on a mission entrusted to them by Thomas Jefferson, president of the United States. Lewis and Clark's goal was to find a water route across America to the Pacific Ocean. Jefferson called the mission the Corps of Discovery because he wanted to learn everything possible about the Louisiana Territory, the enormous tract of

Members of the Lewis and Clark expedition are attacked by bears—one of many dangers they encountered during their extensive tour of the Louisiana Territory.

land lying west of the Mississippi River and extending to the Rocky Mountains.

The Lewis and Clark expedition was a remarkable achievement. The sheer adventure of it catches the imaginations of people today, just as it did two hundred years ago. But daring deeds alone did not make the story endure. Readers are still fascinated by the bond of friendship that developed between the two captains, by Sacagawea's joyful reunion with her family, by the loyalty and cheerfulness of the men, by acts of kindness that occurred between Indians and expedition members, by the beauty and bounty of the land as described by Lewis in his journals—and so much more. If the story were fiction, it would seem too unrealistic.

But the story is not fiction. It was recorded daily in field notebooks and journals by Lewis or Clark or both over a period of two years. Some of the enlisted men also kept journals. The expedition is probably one of the most carefully recorded events in American history.

The story begins, not on the wild frontier, but in the mind of a remarkable man, Thomas Jefferson. The Corps of Discovery was his special project, shaped by his own personality, and by what was happening in North America at the beginning of the nineteenth century.

1 The Lewis and Clark Expedition: Its Roots and Purposes

Historians differ over what was in Thomas Jefferson's mind in February 1801 when he wrote a letter asking Captain Meriwether Lewis to become his private secretary. Jefferson had just been elected president of the United States and needed an assistant. Lewis was serving as paymaster of the First Infantry Regiment at Pittsburgh.

Historian Bernard DeVoto believes that Jefferson picked Lewis to be his secretary because he had already decided to send him on an expedition west of the Mississippi River. DeVoto says Lewis was

> uniquely qualified for a project which Jefferson had cherished for many years, the exploration of the Missouri River and the lands west of its source. Obviously, Jefferson entered office determined to carry out the project as soon as possible and took Lewis into his personal and official household for that purpose.[1]

Indeed, DeVoto's statement seems to be supported by Jefferson's letter, which reads in part, "Your knolege [Jefferson's spelling] of the Western Country, of the army and all of its interests and relations have rendered it desireable for public as well as private purposes that you should be engaged in that office."[2]

Another historian, David Lavender, disagrees with DeVoto's conclusion, however. In contending that Jefferson had no plans for an expedition when he hired Lewis, Lavender says:

> Why did he hire Meriwether Lewis? The reasons were immediate, pragmatic [businesslike], and political.

Thomas Jefferson's foresight led to the exploration of the Missouri River and Louisiana Territory. This remarkable expedition would forever change the future of the United States.

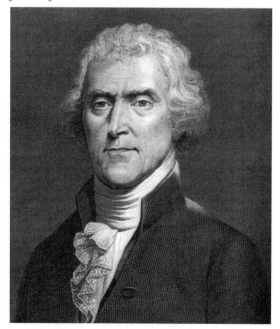

Dressed in a dark uniform crisscrossed with white belts, and wearing a cocked hat with an eagle medallion in its front, the captain would lend dignity to the confidential messages he carried. He could serve as a decorative and charming host at presidential dinners—a real need for Jefferson was a widower and his daughters could not often leave their households to help. More important, Lewis was a stalwart Republican [dedicated member of the same political party as Jefferson].[3]

Which theory is the correct one we shall never know. What we do know is that two years after becoming Jefferson's secretary, Meriwether Lewis was off on the greatest adventure of his life, an adventure

Army captain Meriwether Lewis (pictured) became Thomas Jefferson's private secretary in 1801. Shortly thereafter, Lewis would become one of America's most well-known explorers.

that would place his name among those of the most honored explorers in American history.

Why Jefferson Organized the Expedition

Jefferson had many reasons for wanting to send an expedition to the Pacific Ocean. One of these was a deep curiosity about what lay in the unexplored lands west of the Mississippi River. Before becoming president, Jefferson had supported two separate, and unsuccessful, attempts to explore the western country. He even had approached Revolutionary War hero George Rogers Clark (an older brother of William Clark) about undertaking such a trip, but Clark was unable to go at that time.

After his inauguration in March 1801, Jefferson was ready to try again. This time he had the resources and the authority to organize an expedition. There was so much he wanted to know. He was anxious to learn about the botany (plants), zoology (animals), and geography of the West. He was curious about the customs and languages of the Indians.

Of course, it was not only curiosity that prompted the expedition. Serious political issues also influenced Jefferson's decision. One of these had to do with control of the Louisiana Territory.

In 1800, the Mississippi River was the western boundary of the United States. Spain claimed the Louisiana Territory, which lay west of the river. However, many Americans, including Jefferson, expected that this vast region would eventually become part of the United States. The Span-

Jefferson's Curiosity About the Louisiana Territory

Jefferson was eager to know what natural resources lay in the Louisiana Territory. In June 1803, he sent a letter to Lewis with a list of things to observe while on the expedition. This excerpt is reported in The Way to the Western Sea: Lewis and Clark Across the Continent *by David Lavender.*

"Other objects worthy of notice will be—the soil & face of the country, it's growth and vegetable productions, especially those not of the United States; The animals of the country generally, & especially those not known in the United States; The remains and accounts of any which may be deemed rare or extinct; The mineral productions of every kind, but more particularly metals, lime-stone, pit-coal, and saltpetre; salines and mineral waters, noting the temperature of the last, and such circumstances as may indicate their character; volcanic appearances; Climate as characterized by the thermometer, by the proportion of rainy, cloudy & clear days; by lightning, hail, snow, ice; by the access and recess of frost; by the winds prevailing at different seasons . . . the dates at which particular plants put forth or lose their leaves . . . times of appearance of particular birds, reptiles, or insects."

ish empire in the New World had grown so large that Spain could no longer control or defend all of it.

It was in the best interests of the United States, therefore, to learn as much as possible about the Louisiana Territory. Did the Missouri River run all the way to the sea? How high were the mountains? What minerals and other resources did the territory have? Was farm land available? What kinds of animals inhabited the territory? Were the Indians friendly or hostile?

The desire to establish contact with the Indians west of the Mississippi was another important reason for sending the expedition. Powerful tribes were known to exist along the Missouri River, which was an area rich in furs. British fur traders from Canada were trying to expand their business into the Louisiana Territory. To keep the British out, and perhaps to cash in on the profitable fur trade as well, the United States needed to gain the friendship and loyalty of the Indian tribes as soon as possible. In his letter of instructions to Meriwether Lewis in 1803, Jefferson said:

Treat them [the Indians] in the most friendly & conciliatory [peaceful] manner which their own conduct will admit; Allay [lessen] all jealousies as to the object of your journey, satisfy them of its innocence, make them acquainted with the position, extent, character, peaceable and commercial dispositions [intentions] of the U.S. of our wish to be neighborly, friendly &

useful to them, & of our dispositions to a commercial intercourse [trade] with them . . . [and] if a few of their influential chiefs, within practicable distance, wish to visit us, arrange such a visit with them . . . [and] if any of them should wish to have their young people brought up with us, & taught such arts as may be useful to them, we will receive, instruct, & take care of them.[4]

Indians living east of the Mississippi River were also of concern to Jefferson, but in a different way. By 1800 tribes along the Atlantic seacoast had lost most of their lands to white settlers, and now large numbers of pioneers were crossing the Appalachian Mountains into Indian territory on the frontier. As a result, violence and bloodshed between the two groups were increasing.

Jefferson believed both Indians and settlers could find room in the new nation. In 1803 he wrote to a frontier army officer saying, "In truth, the ultimate point of rest & happiness for them [the Indians] is to let our settlements and theirs meet and blend together, to intermix, and become one people."[5]

Like most Americans of his day, however, Jefferson expected the Indians to do all the changing. He wanted them to settle down on farms so they would not need so much land. If that didn't work, perhaps Indians who insisted on keeping their hunting lifestyle could move into the Louisiana Territory. In a letter to William H. Harrison, governor of the Indiana Territory, Jefferson wrote, "our settlements will gradually circumscribe [encircle] and approach the Indians, and they will in time either incorporate with us as citizens of the United States, or remove beyond the Mississippi."[6]

Congress Approves the Expedition

With so much to be gained by exploring the lands west of the Mississippi, Jefferson decided to ask Congress to authorize an expedition into the Louisiana Territory regardless of who claimed it. On January 18, 1803, he sent a secret message to Congress asking for funding for a scientific expedition to be led by his secretary, Meriwether Lewis. He would seek Spain's permission later. Congress approved, and Lewis began to make preparations.

It was then that an unexpected event took place that changed the nature of the expedition and made it more important than ever. That event was the purchase by the United States of the Louisiana Territory from France, to whom Spain had secretly transferred these lands.

The Louisiana Purchase

Napoleon Bonaparte had recently come to power in France. Years before, France had lost all its holdings in North America and now Napoleon, a strong military leader, wanted them back. He had begun his campaign peacefully enough, by persuading Spain to return the Louisiana Territory, which France had given to Spain in 1762 to keep Great Britain from getting it at the end of the French and Indian Wars.

The news of the soon-to-be-completed transfer greatly worried Jefferson. France was a much more powerful and aggressive nation than Spain and could pose a threat to the newly formed United States. Napoleon had already established a foothold in North America. By a treaty with Spain in 1795, he gained possession of the Caribbean island of Hispaniola (today the countries of Haiti and the Dominican Republic). Many years before, France had established a sugar producing colony on the west end of Hispaniola operated by slave labor. In 1791, under the leadership of Toussaint L'Ouverture, the slaves rebelled and expelled the French. In 1802, Napoleon dispatched twenty-thousand troops across the ocean to retake the rebellious colony and to establish Hispaniola as his base of operations in the New World. When that had been accomplished, he intended to occupy the Louisiana Territory, which included the port of New Orleans.

In a separate incident in 1802, the Spanish commander in New Orleans closed the port to American shipping. This was a serious blow to farmers on the frontier, who brought their products down the river to New Orleans for reshipment to other markets.

Because it was known that Spain was in the process of transferring the Louisiana Territory to France, many settlers thought Napoleon had closed the port. Actually, Napoleon had nothing to do with the closing, and the port was reopened several months later. Nevertheless, the incident made it very clear that the United States needed to own New Orleans. It was not in U.S. interests for any European country to be able to close the port for any reason.

To avoid the possibility of another port closing when France took over the Louisiana Territory, many Americans wanted to go to war with Napoleon immediately. Jefferson, however, was determined to solve the matter through diplomacy if he could. He instructed Robert Livingston,

the American ambassador in Paris, to try to buy the port of New Orleans. As directed, Livingston began negotiations with Charles Maurice de Talleyrand, Napoleon's minister of foreign affairs. Talleyrand did not like America, and for weeks, Livingston's efforts to make a deal were unsuccessful.

Early in the morning of April 11, 1803, Napoleon called his finance minister, François Barbé-Marbois, to his living quarters. Napoleon was distressed. His scheme of returning France to power in the New World was not going well. Thousands of the soldiers he had sent to the Caribbean had been killed in combat or had died from yellow fever. Moreover, he needed money to wage his wars in Europe.

Although a strong military leader, Napoleon Bonaparte's financial difficulties took precedence over his campaign to regain the Louisiana Territory.

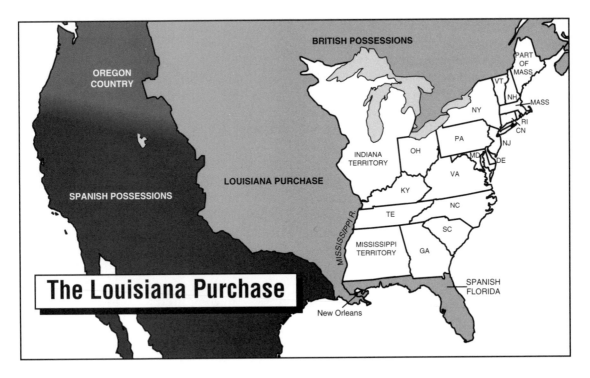

The Louisiana Purchase

To Marbois, Napoleon said, "I renounce Louisiana. It is not only New Orleans that I cede; it is the whole colony, without reserve. . . . I know the price of what I abandon. . . . I renounce it with greatest regret; to attempt obstinately [stubbornly] to retain it would be folly. I direct you to negotiate the affair. Have an interview this very day with Mr. Livingston."[7]

A few hours later, Talleyrand met with Ambassador Livingston, whom he completely surprised by asking what the United States would be willing to pay for the entire Louisiana Territory. Livingston said he needed time to consult with James Monroe, then ambassador to Spain, who had just arrived in Paris.

When Livingston told Monroe about the offer, the future president was greatly surprised, too. Jefferson had instructed his ambassadors to buy only New Orleans (from France) and perhaps Western

Florida (from Spain). Yet the diplomats were unable to ask Jefferson what to do because it took six weeks for mail to travel from Paris to Washington. Using their own judgment, the two ambassadors decided to accept the offer. After many days of bargaining over terms and price, Monroe and Livingston signed a treaty on May 2, 1803 (but dated April 30), in which the United States agreed to pay fifteen million dollars for the entire Louisiana Territory.

President Jefferson received unofficial news of the Louisiana Purchase on July 3, 1803, just in time for the Fourth of July celebration the next day. The treaty itself arrived on July 14. Jefferson immediately wrote of the acquisition to Captain Lewis, who was on his way to Pittsburgh to have a keelboat made for the coming expedition. When Lewis received the letter on July 22, he, too, was very pleased. Now he would be exploring in his own country.

Napoleon Decides to Sell the Louisiana Territory

When Napoleon offered to sell Louisiana to the United States, it came as such a surprise to Robert Livingston, America's ambassador to France, that he said no at first. After thinking about it briefly, he changed his mind. Livingston later wrote to James Madison about the event.

"M. Talleyrand [Napoleon's minister of foreign affairs] asked me this day, when pressing the subject, whether we wished to have the whole of Louisiana. I told him no; that our wishes extended only to New Orleans and the Floridas; . . . He said that if they gave New Orleans the rest would be of little value, and that he would wish to know 'what we would give for the whole.' I told him it was a subject I had not thought of, but that I supposed we should not object to twenty million [francs]. . . . He told me that this was too low an offer, and that he would be glad if I would reflect upon it and tell him tomorrow. I told him that Mr. Monroe [James Monroe, another American ambassador] would be in town in two days, I would delay my further offer until I had the pleasure of introducing him."

Effects of the Louisiana Purchase on the Expedition

Although the Louisiana Purchase was not the original reason for the Lewis and Clark expedition (as is often supposed), the transfer of land ownership made official arrangements for the project less difficult. Jefferson no longer had to seek permission from Spain or France to explore the territory. He no longer had to pretend that it was purely a scientific expedition, but could openly include political and commercial goals as well. Owning the territory made it more important than ever to learn what the western country was like and what resources it held.

Originally, to keep from arousing Spain's suspicions, the exploring party was

On May 2, 1803, the U.S. ambassadors to France and Spain, Robert Livingston and James Monroe, sign the treaty for the Louisiana Purchase in the presence of French finance minister François Barbé-Marbois.

Lieutenant William Clark, a veteran of the Indian wars and longtime friend of Captain Lewis, was chosen to help command the expedition.

Fort Greenville, Ohio, to join a rifle company commanded by Lieutenant Clark.

As it turned out, the choice of Clark was a good one. Although he and Lewis had very different personalities, they got along very well. Both were young—Lewis was twenty-nine years old and Clark was thirty-three when the expedition began. Both were well suited for the journey, having spent much of their early lives outdoors in the fields and forests. As trained army officers, both were experienced at commanding men, and Clark was a veteran of the frontier Indian wars.

The Stage Is Set

The stage was now set for one of the most famous explorations in American history. Not only would the curiosity of Jefferson (and other scholars) be satisfied, but the political and commercial interests of the United States would be promoted. Questions about the worth of the newly acquired territory would be answered. (Some Americans thought the government had squandered money on a worthless tract of wilderness.) Last, but very important, the expedition would serve notice to the great powers of Europe that the United States of America was becoming a strong nation, capable of looking after its own interests.

to be limited to twelve to fifteen men. Now it could be a larger, better equipped operation. As the size of the project grew, Jefferson thought it would be wise to have a second officer along in case something happened to Captain Lewis on the long journey. For that position, Lewis chose his friend William Clark, whom he had known since 1795, when Lewis was sent to

2 The Corps of Discovery: Getting Ready to Go

As soon as Congress had approved Jefferson's request for an expedition into the Louisiana Territory, Meriwether Lewis began to prepare for it. First of all, he had to study some botany, zoology, and geography. He had to know how to treat injuries and illnesses that might befall him or his men. So that he would know where the expedition was at all times, he had to learn to use navigational instruments, as well, to measure latitude and longitude. This knowledge would permit Lewis to draw accurate maps, not only to ensure the return of his own expedition but for the benefit of later explorers. It turned out that almost all the maps of the expedition's journey were done by William Clark, but it was only common sense to be sure that both captains had the necessary skills.

In March 1803, Jefferson sent Lewis to Philadelphia to learn as much as possible about these matters in a short time. Philadelphia was chosen because it was the center of learning in the United States in 1800. Lewis spent several weeks there studying with outstanding scientists who were also friends of Jefferson's. Writing about the time Lewis spent in Philadelphia, Dr. E. G. Chuinard says:

> Thomas Jefferson had the utmost confidence in Meriwether Lewis, including his capacity to absorb important information and its significance. Although

The compass that William Clark used during the expedition. Such instruments allowed Lewis and Clark to navigate their way through unknown territories, and aided in the drawing of accurate maps for later explorers.

Lewis had no formal training in certain requisites [requirements] for his future responsibilities, Jefferson knew that with minimal [little] instruction he would rapidly acquire all the knowledge and technique not already familiar to him.

To better equip Lewis for the . . . responsibilities as leader of the expedition, Jefferson requested assistance from certain of his friends . . . in . . . Philadelphia. . . . Letters of introduction went to Benjamin Smith Barton, a physician but also a botanist—to Caspar Wistar, also a physician and professor of anatomy . . . and to Robert Patterson, professor of medicine. . . .

Dr. Benjamin Rush (pictured) instructed Lewis about medicines and treatment of illnesses in case members of the expedition became ill during the long journey.

These men were to combine their instructions to provide Lewis with the basic information and techniques in taking longitude and latitude and in properly describing and classifying plants and animals.[8]

Jefferson contacted another friend in Philadelphia, Benjamin Rush, a well-known physician. From Dr. Rush, Lewis learned about medicines and the treatment of illnesses. One of the medical techniques Lewis learned was bloodletting. In those days, before scientists had discovered that germs cause diseases, many doctors felt that illnesses were due to morbidity (impurity) of the blood. Thus a popular remedy for fevers and many other illnesses was to make a small cut in a patient's vein and let out some of the bad blood! On the expedition, Lewis used this technique several times on members of the party who became ill.

Lewis Buys Supplies

Lewis also needed to buy supplies for the journey. This was not an easy task because the expedition was going into unknown territory, and no one knew how long the trip would take. Even the exact number of people was undecided until the last minute. Using his best judgment, Lewis bought everything that might possibly be needed, including medicines, tools, rope, firearms, ammunition, blankets, clothing, kettles, tin cups, writing paper, pens, and much more. In Philadelphia, he had 193 pounds of portable (canned) soup made and packed in lead canisters. After the soup had been eaten, the canisters could be melted down to make bullets.

"Portable Soup" for the Expedition

One type of food item Lewis purchased for the expedition was "portable soup," a dried or jellied mixture that would not spoil. This soup later helped save the expedition from starvation. In his book, Only One Man Died: The Medical Aspects of the Lewis and Clark Expedition, *Dr. E. G. Chuinard gives a recipe.*

"An important purchase . . . was '193 lbs. of Portable Soup.' This portable soup was contained in lead canisters and may have been either a dry powder or a thick liquid substance. There is no known record of its exact composition; however, it probably was very similar to the portable soups used by armed forces of the time. [Edward] Cutbush [author of a book about health in the army and navy in 1808] describes the preparation of a portable soup. . . . Take calves' feet, 4; the lean part of a rump of beef 12 pounds; fillet of veal 3 pounds; leg of mutton 10 pounds. These are to be boiled in a sufficient quantity of water and the scum taken off. When the meat becomes very tender, the liquid is to be separated from it by expression [pressing]; and when cold, the fat must be carefully taken off. The jelly-like substance must then be dissolved over the fire and clarified with five or six whites of eggs [any remaining little pieces of meat would be trapped in the egg whites and could be discarded]. It is then to be salted to the taste and boiled down to the consistency of paste, when it is to be poured out on a marble table and cut into pieces, either round or square, and dried in a stove room. When perfectly hard, they should be put up in close vessels of tine [tin] or glass. Powdered rice, beans, peas, barley, celery . . . may be added; but for the use of the sick it should be made plain. . . .

Cutbush also gives directions for using the portable soup: To make soup from this article, one or two cakes must be dissolved in a pint of boiling water to which may be added two or three teaspoons of powdered rice, or whole rice boiled soft; then add a little dry celery powder or parsley; sometimes a little salt, pepper, cloves, and wine may be added. . . . If the portable soup be of the consistency of a jelly, in a canister, one tablespoon will be sufficient for a pint of water. It should never be boiled; as it renders the whole unpleasant, and gives it the taste of glue."

Lewis also bought such items as calico shirts, beads, rings, ribbons, small bells, brooches, earrings, looking glasses, needles, knives, and tomahawks, to give to the Indians along the way.

Lewis purchased many of the supplies while he was studying in Philadelphia, particularly medicines and scientific instruments, like compasses, thermometers, and measuring devices. Other supplies, such as rifles and ammunition, were purchased from the U.S. Arsenal at Harpers Ferry, Virginia. He made arrangements for all these supplies to be shipped by wagon to Pittsburgh, where they would be loaded on a riverboat for the trip to St. Louis.

Prior to beginning the arduous expedition, Lewis purchased numerous provisions, ranging from cooking utensils (above) to rifles and telescopes (below).

Other provisions, such as flour, salt, meal, and salt pork were to be purchased later at St. Louis.

In April 1803, Lewis returned to Washington to take care of last-minute details and to say goodbye to family and friends. On July 5 he left Washington, going first to Harpers Ferry, where a collapsible iron boat frame was being prepared for him. The boat frame was Lewis's invention, which he believed might come in handy on the expedition. The frame was designed to be fitted together quickly and covered with bark or animal hides. Lewis named his custom-built prototype *Experiment*. After making arrangements for the boat frame, rifles, ammunition, and other supplies to be shipped to Pittsburgh by wagon, he continued to that city by horseback.

Lewis Has a Keelboat Made at Pittsburgh

According to the president's letter of instructions, the object of Lewis's mission was "to explore the Missouri river, & such principal stream of it, as, by it's course & communication with the waters of the Pacific Ocean, may offer the most direct & practicable water communication across this continent, for the purposes of commerce."[9] That a man as well informed as Thomas Jefferson thought the Missouri River or any of its "principal streams" ran into the Pacific Ocean is definite proof of the need for the proposed exploration. In any event, the president's goal was to map out a direct route to the ocean, and he accepted the possibility that some land travel might be necessary.

Lewis, for his part, was aware that the Missouri River was wide and powerful in its lower reaches, and he knew that his party would be traveling against the current. Thus he had to have a large, well-constructed boat. Lewis had made arrangements for a keelboat to be built at Pittsburgh. Much to his disappointment when he arrived, he learned that the work had barely begun. The boat contractor was undependable and often drank too much. With Lewis there to hurry him on, however, the work went forward more swiftly.

The blueprint for the keelboat to be used by the Corps of Discovery. This flat-bottomed cargo boat was 55 feet long, had one square sail, and 20 oars for rowing upstream.

Keelboats were flat-bottomed cargo boats commonly used on America's rivers before steamboats were invented. They had many sets of oars for rowing upstream, and usually carried a small sail as well. In addition to oars, long wooden poles were used to push the vessels in shallow water. Sometimes the keelboats were towed by men or horses walking ahead, along the bank.

The keelboat of the Corps of Discovery had twenty oars, ten on each side. Historian John Bakeless describes it as follows:

> The keelboat was the kind of craft which both of the officers [Lewis and Clark] and many of the soldiers had used on the Ohio—55 feet long, drawing three feet of water [extending three feet below water], and carrying one square sail. She was decked over for ten feet in the bow [front], with a cabin astern [in the back]. Along the gunwales [sides] amidships, lockers were placed so their lids could be raised to give additional protection in case of attack.[10]

Lewis and Clark Select Members of the Expedition

Before the Louisiana Purchase, the number of expedition members was set at no more than fifteen men. Jefferson thought it best to keep the group small so as not to upset Spain (or France) in whose territory they would be traveling. After the Louisiana Territory became part of the United States, there was no longer any need for secrecy and the size of the expedition greatly increased. Safety was another reason for the addition. The expedition needed to be large enough to defend itself in case any of the natives were unfriendly.

While waiting in Pittsburgh for the keelboat to be finished, Lewis began interviewing volunteers who wanted to become members of the expedition. The Corps of Discovery was a military operation, so some of its members were chosen from regular army troops; others enlisted in the army after being selected. A few civilians (nonsoldiers) were later employed for special jobs, such as interpreter and boatman.

In the interviews, Lewis looked for strong men (preferably unmarried) who had special skills such as hunting, blacksmithing, or carpentry. He wanted men who could get along well with others, men who were used to working hard in the outdoors and would obey orders. To attract men with these qualities, some kind of encouragement had to be given. Historian Charles G. Clarke says:

> While the men were selected with great care, Captain Lewis was authorized to offer the following inducements [rewards] to those enlisting:
>
> First: . . . six months pay in advance. Pay of $10.00 per month, plus clothing and subsistence [any expenses connected with food and shelter].
>
> Second: To discharge them from service if they wish it, immediately on their return from the expedition, giving them their arrears of pay, clothing, etc.
>
> Third: To secure them a portion of land equal to that given by the United States to the officers and soldiers who served in the Revolutionary War.[11]

George Drouillard, Expedition Member

One of the outstanding members of the expedition was George Drouillard (usually spelled Drewer or Drewyer in the journals). He was the son of a French-Canadian father and a Shawnee mother. Unlike most of the other members, he was not a soldier. In this excerpt from George Drouillard: Hunter and Interpreter for Lewis and Clark, *M.O. Skarsten describes Drouillard's excellent qualities.*

"When Lewis and Clark engaged George Drouillard as interpreter for the expedition which they proposed to lead to the Pacific, they transacted a piece of business that yielded them returns beyond their most sanguine [hopeful] expectations; and this for the reason that George Drouillard was to demonstrate to them an ability and a willingness to serve them, not merely in the capacity of interpreter, but in several other capacities as well.

For example, George Drouillard proved himself invaluable as a hunter. He demonstrated more than ordinary success in diplomatic ventures to the Indians. He became a boon [close] companion of Lewis. . . .

A cursory [brief] examination of the accomplishments of George Drouillard in behalf of the Lewis and Clark expedition will disclose that here lived a man of strong yet nimble physique [body build], equally at home in the woods, on the plains, and in the mountains; a man of quick decision and vigorous action; enthusiastic, ardent [intense], courageous, resourceful, likeable. It was the all-out competence of the man, his willingness—nay, even eagerness—to serve on any occasion, his unfailing reliability, his courage, tact, good judgment, and resourcefulness—it was qualities such as these that served, singly and in combination, to make him well-nigh indispensable [necessary] in the furtherance of the project to which he had committed himself. Of him it can truthfully be said: He ranked high among those energetic, gallant men whose claim to recognition lay in the fact that they served with honor and distinction the expedition commanded by Lewis and Clark; and, in so doing, the country to which they owed allegiance."

From the many volunteers interviewed, Lewis selected only three men on a trial basis. Meanwhile, in Louisville, Clark was also interviewing volunteers.

"With William Clark's agreement to join Captain Lewis in the expedition," writes Charles G. Clarke, "Lewis advised him to be on the lookout for suitable men.

Several young gentlemen's sons applied to Clark, but as he felt they were not accustomed to labor, he had to diplomatically [tactfully] offer them no encouragement."[12] Both captains understood that the successful completion of their mission depended upon the selection of a courageous, skillful, and trustworthy crew.

Down the Ohio River

With the crew selection underway (but far from complete), Lewis began the trip down the Ohio River in the new keelboat. On August 31, 1803, he wrote, "Left Pittsburgh this day at 11 [o'clock] with a party of 11 hands [crewmen] 7 of which are soldiers, a pilot [river guide] and three young men on trial they having proposed to go with me throughout the voyage."[13] Also on board the new keelboat was a dog Lewis had recently purchased. It was a large black Newfoundland named Seaman (often called Scannon from a misreading of the handwriting in the journals).

Today, a direct flight from Pittsburgh, where the keelboat was constructed, to St. Louis, the expedition's official starting point, covers only about six hundred miles. The water route, however, is far longer. The stretch of the Ohio River that lies between Pittsburgh and St. Louis makes many loops and turns and this preliminary leg of Lewis's journey was itself a major undertaking.

Navigating the keelboat was difficult at first, but after a time, the river grew deeper and the vessel was easier to handle. In October at Clarksville in the Indiana Territory (near Louisville, Kentucky),

Lewis was reunited with his friend and former commanding officer, William Clark. Nearly two weeks later, with the second captain now aboard, the party continued down the Ohio to the Mississippi River, which they had to cross to begin their journey on the Missouri.

By the end of November, the keelboat was getting close to St. Louis, an important frontier town founded by the French on the west bank of the Mississippi River. Since the northern part of the Louisiana Territory (called Upper Louisiana) had not yet been officially transferred to the United States, the expedition stayed on the east side of the river.

Arrival at Winter Camp

In early December Captain Lewis left Clark in charge of the keelboat and crossed over to St. Louis. There he paid his respects to Spain's lieutenant governor, Carlos Delassus, who was still in charge of Upper Louisiana. In the meantime, Clark proceeded up the river with the keelboat and crew. A winter campsite was selected opposite the spot where the Missouri River flows into the Mississippi, about eighteen miles north of St. Louis. On one side of the campsite a little river, named the *Rivière Dubois* by the French ("Wood River" in English), flows into the Mississippi. So the site was called Camp Dubois or Camp Wood.

The weather was already getting cold, so Clark immediately started making winter camp: "fixed on a place to build huts Set the Men to Clearing land & Cutting Logs," he wrote on December 13, 1803. In later entries he noted,

While in St. Louis (pictured), Clark acquired additional supplies, hired boatmen, and made official appearances on behalf of the Corps of Discovery.

I cut a road to the priary 2490 yards East Commenc the Cabins. . . . rais one Cabin at night. . . . a raney day continue to put up my huts the men much fatigued Carrying logs.[14]

(The daily journals were often written hastily under difficult conditions, so the writers did not always take time to use commas and periods. Also, none of the writers except Captain Lewis had been trained in spelling and writing.) He also told of buying provisions such as turnips, corn, and butter from neighboring farmers. He listed the numbers of deer and wild turkey the hunters brought in each day.

While they waited for spring, Lewis spent the greater part of his time in St. Louis, buying additional supplies, hiring boatmen, making official appearances, and enjoying the hospitality of the leading citi-zens. Clark usually stayed at Camp Wood, overhauling the keelboat, drilling the men, and supervising the work of the camp. Once in a while, they traded places to give Clark a break from the routine of camp.

Because the number of men going on the expedition had increased, two additional boats were obtained. The new boats, called pirogues (peai-ROGUE) were smaller than the keelboat and of a different type. They resembled canoes in shape but were much longer and wider. One of the new pirogues had six oars and was painted white. The other, painted red, had a seventh oar which served as a rudder to steer the vessel. Both pirogues were equipped with masts and sails to use when the wind was favorable.

During the winter, Lewis and Clark read and studied everything about the western country they could get their hands on. They were especially interested in the few maps that were available. They talked with trappers and traders who had traveled part way up the Missouri River. From them they obtained information about the land through which they would travel and about the Indian tribes they might meet.

Clark's Military Commission

Although almost everything else went well that winter, William Clark suffered a big disappointment. He had retired from the army as a lieutenant in the late 1790s, but Lewis, who had served under Clark's command, had remained in the service, eventually rising to the rank of captain. Lewis thought it would be embarrassing to have a higher rank than his old commanding officer, so he had promised Clark the rank of captain while on the expedition.

Unfortunately, the War Department officials in Washington did not agree that Clark should receive this rank. Disappointed with the War Department's decision, Lewis sent a letter to Clark at Camp Wood which said in part:

> My dear friend, I send you herewith inclosed your commission accompanyed by the Secretary of War's letter; it is not such as I wished, or had reason to expect; but so it is—a further explaneation when I join you. I think it will be best to let none of our party or any other persons know any thing about the grade, you will observe that the grade has no effect upon your compensation [pay], which by G—d, shall be equal to my own.[15]

Clark never mentioned the matter to anyone and Lewis kept his word, too. The men of the expedition never knew the difference. Both officers were addressed as "Captain," and all important decisions were made by them jointly throughout the journey.

The lower half of the Louisiana Territory was transferred from France to the United States on December 20, 1803, in New Orleans. Several weeks later, two ceremonies were held in St. Louis transferring Upper Louisiana to the United States. At the first ceremony on March 9, 1804, the territory was conveyed from Spain to

The U.S. flag is raised over New Orleans on December 20, 1803, symbolizing the transfer of the lower half of the Louisiana Territory from France to the United States.

Lewis Writes a Letter to His Mother

In his last letter to his mother before leaving on the expedition, Meriwether Lewis carefully plays down the dangers of his coming journey. Having outlived two husbands and raised several children in the backwoods of Virginia, Lucy Marks probably was not fooled. Here is the letter, reprinted from Letters of the Lewis and Clark Expedition, *edited by Donald Jackson.*

"Dear Mother, Washington July 2nd 1803

The day after tomorrow I shall set out for the Western Country; I had calculated on the pleasure of visiting you before my departure but circumstances have rendered this impossible; my absence will probably be equal to fifteen or eighteen months; the nature of this expedition is by no means dangerous, my rout [route] will be altogether through tribes of Indians who are perfectly friendly to the United States, therefore consider the chances of life just as much in my favor on this trip as I should conceive them were I to remain at home for the same length of time; the charge of this expedition is honorable to myself, as it is important to my Country. For its fatiegues [hardships] I feel myself perfectly prepared, nor do I doubt my health and strength of constitution to bear me through it; I go with the most perfect preconviction [belief] in my own mind of returning safe and hope therefore that you will not suffer yourself to indulge any anxiety for my safety. . . . I shall write you again on my arrival in Pittsburgh, Adieu [goodbye] and believe me your affectionate son,

Meriwether Lewis"

France. At the second ceremony, held the following day, France transferred the land to the United States. Neither Lewis nor Clark wrote about the ceremonies, but a description has been pieced together from other sources.

Both transfers took place at the Government House in St. Louis. They were conducted with impressive military displays including marching soldiers, drawn sabers, drums, and booming cannons. At the first ceremony, Spain's lieutenant governor, Carlos Delassus, gave a farewell speech. He then signed the official transfer papers along with Captain Amos Stoddard of the United States Army. Jefferson had recently appointed Stoddard as administrator of the Upper Louisiana Territory. At this first ceremony, however, Captain Stoddard acted as the representative for France. At the end of the ceremony, the Spanish flag was lowered and the French flag was raised. Captain Meriwether Lewis served as one of the official witnesses to the transfer.

On the following day, the French transferred Upper Louisiana to the United States. This time, Captain Stoddard acted on behalf of the United States of America. David Lavender describes the scene:

The next morning, March 10, the same crowd gathered for the symbolic ceremony transferring French Louisiana to the United States. [Lieutenant Stephen] Worrell's troops [from U.S. Fort Kaskaskia] . . . marched up Bonhomme Street to stand at attention where the Spanish soldiers had stood the day before. At 10:00 A.M. the same officials, with Clark added this time, stepped outside, Stoddard carrying the Stars and Stripes. Meriwether Lewis and his fellow witnesses stepped forward to testify to the actuality of the transfer, and the little cannon up on the hill boomed out another series of salutes. Upper Louisiana was now legally American.[16]

All Lewis and Clark had to wait for now was the coming of spring. On April 8, when Sergeant John Ordway wrote to his parents telling them about being chosen for the expedition, he said "we are to Start in ten days up the Missouri River."[17] But he was wrong! There was another delay. With the help of Pierre Chouteau, a St. Louis fur trader, Lewis had invited a delegation of Osage Indian chiefs to go to Washington to see the president. (Jefferson instructed Lewis to organize such visits whenever possible.) The Osage group didn't arrive until April 21, however, and then Lewis had to spend many more days making arrangements to send them on to Washington under military escort.

The delays were hard on the crew's morale, and discipline problems erupted.

Some of the men refused to obey the orders of Sergeant Ordway, who was in charge at Camp Wood when the captains were away, and several had to be punished for rule violations. For the most part, however, the crew was an excellent one which proved its worth over and over again in the following months. Most of the problems at Camp Wood were caused by boredom and restlessness.

The Expedition Begins

Captain Clark was tired of waiting, too, and determined to put the expedition under way, no matter how short the first stage. While Lewis was still in St. Louis making plans for the Osage delegation's trip to Washington, Clark sent him a message stating that the expedition would start up the Missouri River on Monday, May 14. They would wait for Lewis at St. Charles. In his diary, Clark wrote:

Monday, May 14th, 1804: Rained the forepart of the day I determined to go as far as St. Charles a french Village 7 Leags. up the Missourie, and wait at that place untill Capt. Lewis could finish the business in which he was obliged to attend to at St. Louis and join me by Land from that place 24 miles; By this movement I calculated that if any alterations in the loading of the Vestles or other Changes necessary, that they might be made at St. Charles.

I set out at 4 oClock P. M. in the presence of many of the Neighbouring inhabitents, and proceeded on under a jentle brease up the Missouri.[18]

Chapter

3 The Journey: From Camp Wood to the Mandan Villages

The diaries and journals kept by several of the men on the expedition do not agree on how many men left Camp Wood on May 14, 1804. David Lavender says:

> Clark gave one set of figures for those in the keelboat; sergeants Ordway, Floyd, and Prior, who had been ordered to keep journals to increase the likelihood that some record would survive in the event of catastrophe, gave variants. . . . The following totals are not far askew [are probably quite close], however: twenty-five including York [Clark's slave], in the keelboat; nine Frenchmen under their *patron* [leader], Baptiste Deschamps, in the

red pirogue, and seven soldiers, including Corporal Warfington, in the smaller, white painted pirogue.[19]

Lavender's list totals forty-one, over three times as many as Jefferson had proposed in his secret message to Congress sixteen months before. But the situation had changed a great deal since January 1803, and now three boatloads of hand-picked, well-armed men were heading up the Missouri River. It was a rocky start. With the breakup of the winter ice, the Missouri was running swiftly. Great numbers of logs and other kinds of driftwood moved rapidly along, threatening to crash into the boats. Another danger lay just un-

Departing from the river city St. Charles (pictured), the Corps of Discovery set forth to explore the Louisiana Territory and the dangerous Missouri River.

derneath the water in the form of broken trees called snags, which could tear the bottom out of a boat. Sometimes the very banks of the river caved in, eroded away by the rushing waters. In addition, the keelboat was badly loaded, causing the craft to handle poorly.

In spite of the dangers, the little fleet arrived safely at St. Charles two days later. While they waited for Captain Lewis, Clark had all the boats reloaded to distribute the weight more evenly. On May 20, Lewis arrived, and the Corps of Discovery left St. Charles the next day. Many residents of the town came down to the river to bid them farewell.

As the expedition slowly made its way up the river, Captain Lewis often stayed ashore, riding one of the expedition's three horses or walking along the banks. He made notes about plants and animals and reckoned the position of landmarks. Usually, three or four hunters stayed ashore also. It took a lot of food to satisfy dozens of men doing hard physical labor every day.

Most of the time, Captain Clark remained aboard the keelboat, keeping a sharp lookout for dangers ahead. And there were plenty of these. In one particularly bad stretch, called the Devil's Race Ground, the river ran swiftly between overhanging rocks on one side and an island on the other. In trying to pass through, the keelboat almost turned over. Clark wrote:

> We *hove* up [moved] near the head of the Sand bar, the Sand moveing & banking caused us to run on the Sand. The Swiftness of the Current wheeled the boat, Broke our *Toe* [tow] rope, and was nearly over Setting [capsizing] the boat, all hand Jumped out on

the upper Side and bore on [upheld] that Side untill the Sand washed from under the boat and Wheeled on the next bank by the time She wheeled a 3rd Time got a rope fast to her Stern and by the means of swimmers was Carried to Shore.[20]

Toiling up the river against the current was exhausting. Although few serious injuries were reported, Clark told of treating men for boils, colds, headaches, and sun stroke. Dysentery, an intestinal illness caused by improper diet and unsanitary conditions, was also a frequent complaint. Mosquitoes, gnats, and ticks were so bad that the captains bought animal grease from a trader to smear on the men's bodies.

Life was not all sickness and hardship, however. The journal writers described the beauty and natural wonders of the land through which they were passing. Wild fruits were ripening along the river—plums, currants, raspberries, and grapes of different kinds. Fishing was excellent and game was plentiful. The hunters killed deer, antelope, elk, beaver, buffalo, goats, and rabbits, which they used for food. When clothes and shoes issued by the army wore out, Corps members replaced them with Indian-style shirts, leggings, and moccasins made from tanned animal hides.

The Captains Hold an Indian Council

On July 22 the party reached the mouth of the Platte River where Omaha, Nebraska, is located today. In 1804 this area was home to the Oto and Missouri tribes. In

When Lewis and Clark reached the mouth of the Platte River on July 22, 1804, the region was inhabited by the Oto and Missouri tribes.

keeping with their mission, Lewis and Clark decided to hold a council. Messengers were sent out to invite the Oto chiefs to the council, but the villages were deserted because people were away on their summer buffalo hunt.

The captains were about to give up on the council when Drouillard happened to meet a Missouri Indian who lived among the Otos. This man agreed to return to his small village and bring back whomever he could find. In the meantime, the expedition moved slowly up the river, waiting for their guests to catch up with them.

On August 2, 1804, a small party of Oto and Missouri Indians arrived, none of them principal chiefs. It was not exactly what the captains had hoped for, but it would have to do. The council took place the next day on a bluff overlooking the Missouri, a few miles north of the Platte River. They named the site Council Bluffs.

The council was held under a canopy made from the sail of the keelboat. The soldiers marched in full uniform to impress their guests. Lewis delivered a speech about the Great Father in Washington (Jefferson), who was chief over seventeen nations (states). Some of the Indians made speeches in return, and then the captains distributed presents and medals with Jefferson's likeness stamped on them.

Lewis demonstrated a new gun that used compressed air instead of gunpowder. It made a loud popping noise. In his journal, Clark noted that the Indians were astonished. At the close of the council, gifts were sent to Little Thief and Big Horse, two principal chiefs who had not attended.

Peace Medals for the Indians

To win the loyalty of the Indians, explorers from Spain, France, and England gave peace medals of silver and bronze to American Indian chiefs. When the United States became an independent nation, the practice of giving peace medals continued. In this excerpt from Indian Peace Medals in American History, *historian Francis Paul Prucha describes the medals distributed by Lewis and Clark.*

"The expedition of Lewis and Clark depended for its success in large measure upon winning the respect and friendship of the Indian tribes encountered along the way. Since many of these Indians . . . had long been conditioned [accustomed] to the presentation of silver peace medals by the agents and traders of France, Spain, and Great Britain, it is unthinkable that Lewis and Clark could have successfully completed their expedition of discovery had they not been prepared to continue the practice that had been so firmly established. They were, in fact, well prepared.

President Jefferson, in his instructions to Lewis of June 20, 1803, told him to apply to the Secretary of War for 'light articles for barter and presents among the Indians,' and it was no doubt through the War Department that Lewis received the peace medals which he took along, although no specific record remains of their requisition or receipt.

At Camp Dubois [Wood], where Lewis and Clark wintered in 1803–1804 while making final preparations for the expedition, the goods which had been accumulated for presentation to the Indians were organized and packed for the journey. . . . There were fourteen bales or bags all told, plus a case. . . .

The first presentation of peace medals by Lewis and Clark occurred on Friday, August 3, 1804, when the expedition was camped at Council Bluffs. . . . The chiefs were admonished [strongly advised] to turn in to their great father [Jefferson] all the flags and medals they had received from the French and the Spanish in exchange for new ones."

A replica of the silver peace medals that were distributed during the expedition.

Deserters in the Ranks

As the expedition continued up the river, Private Moses Reed asked permission to return to the last camp to look for a knife he had left there. Sergeant Floyd recorded the incident on August 7:

> On the 4th of this month one of ouer men by the name of Moses B. Reed went Back to ouer Camp whare we had Left in the morning, to Git his Knife which he Had Left at the Camp the Boat went on and He Did not Return, that night nor the next day nor Night, pon examining his nap-Sack we found that he had taken his Cloas and all His powder and Balles, and had hid them out that night and had made an excuse to Desarte [desert] from us with out aney Jest Case [just cause].[21]

Liberté, a French boatman sent to the Oto village on an errand, had not returned either. Convinced that he and Reed had deserted, Clark sent Drouillard and three soldiers back to find them. If Little Thief and Big Horse had returned from the buffalo hunt, Drouillard and his party were to invite them to a council.

At the Oto village, Reed was captured, but Liberté escaped. Little Thief and Big Horse were there, and they accepted Clark's invitation. Traveling together, both groups arrived at the expedition's camp on August 18.

After welcoming their visitors, Lewis and Clark proceeded to hold a court-martial for the captured deserter. Moses Reed was found guilty and sentenced to run the gauntlet four times. This meant running between two rows of soldiers who struck the prisoner on his bare back with switches. When Little Thief and Big Horse saw what was going to happen to Reed, they protested. They could not imagine humiliating a member of their own tribe in that way.

Lewis and Clark explained to them that desertion was a very serious offense in a military company. Clark wrote, "After we explained the injurey Such men could doe them by false representation, & explang. the Customs of our Countrey they were all Satisfied with the propriety [rightness] of the Sentence & was witness to the punishment."[22]

After the court-martial, any bad feelings were quickly overcome when expedition member Pierre Cruzatte played his fiddle, and the men began dancing. Clark noted that the merriment went on until eleven o'clock.

The next day, Lewis and Clark held a council for the chiefs and their party. They also invited chiefs from the Omaha tribe, hoping to bring about peace between the warring Otos and Omahas. Unfortunately, the Omahas were still away hunting buffalo, so the peace conference fell through.

The council did not go well, either. The chiefs, who had expected to receive valuable gifts, were dissatisfied with the trinkets given to them. Moreover, Lewis's speech about the great new chief in Washington didn't impress them. They had grown accustomed to seeing the land change hands among the white men. As long as they got the trade goods they desired, the Indians no longer cared who was in charge. This attitude came as a surprise to Lewis and Clark. According to historian James P. Ronda:

> Lewis and Clark had expected the Indians' quick acceptance of American

policies. All the gifts and military show were aimed at producing that result. On the other hand, the Otos and Missouris imagined wonderful giveaways of valuable goods from what seemed an endless supply on the keelboat. . . . Each expected too much from the other.[23]

The Death of Sergeant Floyd

The next day the expedition continued up the river. Disappointment with the Indian council was soon overshadowed by a tragic event in their own ranks. As Captain Clark recorded it:

[August 19, 1804]. . . . Serjeant Floyd is taken verry bad all at onc. . . . we attempt to relieve him without Success as yet, he gets wordse and we are muc allarmed at his Situation, all attention to him. . . . 20th *August* Monday. . . . I am Dull & heavy been up the greater Part of last night with Serjt. Floyd, who is a[s] bad as he can be to live. . . . we Came [to] make a warm bath for Sergt. Floyd hopeing it would brace him a little, before we could get him in to this bath he expired, with a great deel of composure, haveing Said to me before his death that he was going away and wished me to write a letter——we . . . [took] him to the top of a high round hill over looking the river & Countrey for a great distance Situated just below a Small river without a name to which we name & call Floyds river, the Bluffs Sergts. Floyds Bluff——we buried him with all the honors of War and fixed a Ceeder [cedar] post at his head with his name title & Day of the month and year Capt Lewis read the funeral Service over him after paying everry respect to the Body of this deceased man (who had at All times given us proofs of his impatiality

The hill and river which were named after the deceased Sergeant Floyd. The cedar marker which sits atop the rounded hill commemorates his death.

[unprejudiced nature] and Sincurity [sincerity] to ourselves and good will to Serve his Countrey) we returned to the Boat & proceeded to the Mouth of the little river 30 yd. wide & Camped a butifull evening.[24]

Floyd was the only member of the expedition to die on the journey. Doctors today think he probably had ruptured his appendix. If so, he likely would have died wherever he was, because medical knowledge in 1804 was not advanced enough to deal with such emergencies.

The Corps of Discovery Meets the Sioux

Even though the Oto and Missouri chiefs were displeased, they never threatened the expedition in any way. The Sioux Indians who controlled the river trade on the upper Missouri were another matter. The Sioux were closely allied to the British in Canada, who wanted to control the western river trade themselves. They persuaded the Sioux to trade only with them and to discourage traders who came up the river from St. Louis.

The Sioux were divided into several nations. The first group Lewis and Clark encountered were the Yankton, a band friendlier than some of the others. Lewis sent messengers to invite them to a council on the riverbank. They came in large numbers and had a fine time, dancing and singing. Lewis made his usual speech and the air gun was fired to impress the visitors.

Presents were given out but the Yankton chiefs, too, were dissatisfied. They wanted many more presents, not only for themselves, but to exchange later at a great Indian trade fair held each year on the plains. Through interpreters, Lewis and Clark explained that they were explorers, not traders. The Yankton Sioux let them pass, and they hurriedly moved up the river.

The next group of Sioux, the Tetons, were not as friendly as the Yankton. For a time it appeared that a real shooting match might break out. Sergeant Ordway recorded these alarming events in his diary for Tuesday, September 15, 1804:

a clear and pleasant morning. al things made ready to receive the Band of the Souix nation of Indians, Called the Tribe of Tetons. . . . they came flocking in from boath Sides of the River. . . . Capt Lewis and Capt Clark went out to Speak and treat with them. Gave the 3 Chiefs niew meddals & 1 american flag Some knives & other Small articles of Goods & Gave the head chief the Black Buffalow a red coat & a cocked hat & feather &.C [etc.] likewise some Tobacco. We had no good interpreter but the old frenchman [a trader] could make them understand tollarable well. but they did not appear to talk much untill they had got the goods, and then they wanted more, and Said we must Stop [stay] with them or leave one of the pearogues with them as that was what they expected.

[At this point Lewis and Clark tried to satisfy the Sioux tribal members by demonstrating the air gun, giving more presents, and accepting presents in return]. . . . then the Captains told them that we had a great ways to goe & and that we did not wish to be detained any longer. they [the Indians] then began to act as if they were Intoxicated with Some difficulty Capt Clark got them to Shore. they then began to Show Some Signs of Stopping or attempting to Stop us. . . . the head chief the Black Buffaloe, Seized hold of the cable of the pearogue and Set down. Capt Clark Spoke to all the party to Stand to their arms Capt Lewis who was on board ordered every man to his arms.[25]

Captain Clark and Black Buffalo then engaged in a kind of shouting match about whose nation was the strongest. When Clark refused to back down, Black Buffalo softened his behavior and began to act friendly. For the next two days, the Corps members were treated to feasts and ceremonies by the Tetons, but they never relaxed their guard. Clark reported that he barely slept during those two days.

On September 28, when Lewis and Clark were ready to move on, another attempt was made to stop them. Once more, it appeared that shots might be fired, but the captains again stood firm. After Black Buffalo was given some tobacco for the warriors who were causing trouble, the keelboat was allowed to move on without interference.

The Corps of Discovery was undoubtedly outnumbered during these incidents, and yet the Indians did not press their advantage. As Bernard DeVoto explains it:

A great many of them [the Sioux], however, would have been killed and such a loss was a price they would not pay, which no Indians would pay. . . . According to the Indian conception of warfare, you did not attack a well-armed and resolute enemy. You tried

While camping with the Sioux, Corps members may have witnessed tribal ceremonies such as the Sioux dog feast (pictured).

While traveling through the lands of the Arikara, Mandan, and Hidatsa, the dark skin of York, Clark's slave, astonished the natives who had never seen a black man. Here, the Hidatsa chief curiously examines York's features.

bluff, bluster, and threats. If they did not work, you tried diplomacy and guile [trickery]. . . . If they did not work either, you postponed matters in hope of a more favorable opportunity.[26]

The Corps Reaches the Mandan Villages

Early in October, the travelers reached the land of the Arikara, Mandan, and Hidatsa Indians in present-day North Dakota, sixteen hundred miles from St. Louis. These tribes all had similar cultures. They lived in large, cone-shaped earth lodges. They raised corn, beans, squash, and other crops during the summer. Twice a year they went on a buffalo hunt. All these

tribes had been weakened and reduced in size as a result of smallpox epidemics.

Upon arriving at the Arikara villages, the Corps members were received politely and spent several peaceful days there. Clark had a slave, a man known only as York, who made quite an impression on the Arikaras. Clark notes that "many Came to view us all day, much astonished at my black Servant, who did not lose the opportunity of [displaying] his powers Strength &c. &c. this nation never Saw a black man before. . . . Those people are much pleased with my black Servant."[27] (Clark eventually granted York his freedom and set him up in business.)

Several days later the party moved on to the Mandan villages, where they were welcomed in a friendly manner. After

Who Was York?

"York is a man history has passed by. Instead of being remembered along with other early black Americans who took part in momentous events . . . York is unknown to almost all blacks and whites alike. Yet, as the journals of the expedition testify, this first black man to cross the continent north of Mexico played a meaningful role in one of the most notable explorations in history. . . .

If the modest niche [place] York deserves in American history could be given him merely by reciting his contribution to the expedition, that would be easy enough to do. But the matter becomes somewhat complicated because there are two different Yorks to deal with: the York of the Lewis and Clark journals and the York of myth [legends]. Over the years . . . the York of myth has become the dominant figure, a man of whom more nonsense has been written than any other member of the group including Sacagawea. He has been variously portrayed as a giant of superb physique and stamina; a buffoon [clown] who contributed nothing more than comic relief to the expedition. . . .

When the myths are stripped away, when the depictions [descriptions] of him which were distorted with prejudice are judged for what they are worth . . . a more rounded image of the man takes form. We can see a York much more complex than we have been conditioned to think, a York much more important to the success of the expedition than we have been told, and a York much more tragically a victim of slavery than we have been given to believe."

many difficult miles, the company was still intact, but it was now late in October. They needed to build a shelter in which to pass the harsh northern winter.

Almost immediately after their arrival, the captains and their men set about building a fort on the river bank about a mile below the first Mandan village. Large cottonwood logs were cut and dragged to the site to construct the walls, roof, and fence. By this time the expedition had lost all their horses and had to "hire" one from the Mandans to help hoist the heavy logs into place.

The fort was built in a V shape. Along each arm of the V, four rooms were constructed with a stone fireplace in each room. Above the rooms were lofts for sleeping. Between the arms of the V, there was an open courtyard. A high log fence across the end of the courtyard made the fort triangular in shape. There was also a smokehouse for meat, and a blacksmith shop.

The fort was so well constructed that the residents remained warm even when the river froze and the temperature outside dropped below zero. It must have been a cheerful place, too, because Indians enjoyed coming there. Sometimes the men entertained their guests by dancing while Pierre Cruzatte played his fiddle. On Christmas and New Year's Day, celebrations were held with special food, drink, music, and dancing. In turn, the expedition members were always welcome at the Mandan villages. James P. Ronda says:

> Lewis and Clark's hospitality was well known; Indians often came early in the day, slept overnight in the fort if invited, and left the next morning. . . . Visits from Indian neighbors usually

With the onset of winter, the raging Missouri River would transform itself into a frozen thoroughfare for the Mandans and expedition members.

Fort Mandan

During the winter of 1804, the temperature at the Mandan villages in what is now North Dakota dropped as low as forty degrees below zero on several occasions. In spite of the extreme cold, the men of the expedition stayed warm at Fort Mandan, which they had built with their own hands. In this excerpt from Lewis and Clark: Partners in Discovery, *historian John Bakeless describes the building of Fort Mandan.*

"The site finally selected for Fort Mandan, the expedition's winter quarters, was on the left bank of the Missouri, downstream from the Mandan villages. . . . There was plenty of timber here, and the fort would be near enough to the villages so that the white men could keep an eye on the Indians and also on the Canadian traders, for whom the villages were an important trading center. . . . The men went to work in the wooded bottom lands under the high clay bluffs along the river, felling trees, cutting the logs to length, and flattening a few for the 'puncheons' [logs flattened on one side] used as floor and ceiling of frontier log cabins. . . .

When Fort Mandan was finished, no Sioux war party had any hope of success in attacking it. 'The whole,' said a Canadian observer, 'is made so strong as to be almost cannon ball proof.' It was built in the form of a triangle, or, more accurately a slice of pie. The stout log cabins formed two sides, opening inward. The base of the triangle was closed by a semi-circular stockade. . . .

Fort Mandan was not only strong, it was also warm. The whole expedition moved in about the middle of November to escape the cold, though the cabins were still unfinished. The two commanders shared a separate cabin as living and working quarters, while the men bunked together in small groups."

meant sharing food and enjoying a dance or some fiddle music by Pierre Cruzatte. . . . Social calling was a two-way affair during the winter with the Mandans. Members of the expedition managed to make frequent trips to the Mandan villages. Those trips were usually for trade and occasionally for personal affairs, but some were simply for good company. . . . These visits were a regular part of the explorers' lives during an otherwise difficult winter.[28]

The captains kept very busy that long winter, too. Clark drew maps of where they had been, and Lewis worked on reports to send to Jefferson in the spring. Both captains learned all they could from Indians and visiting traders about the land through which they would be traveling.

Sometimes they had to smooth over complaints from local chiefs, who doubted that the Americans would be able to supply the trade goods they promised. Again and again the captains reminded the Indians that the future of the tribes was tied to that of the United States, not to Great Britain or its dominion in Canada.

The Captains Hire the Charbonneau Family

One day during the stay at Fort Mandan, a man by the name of Toussaint Charbonneau came to see Lewis and Clark. He lived among the Indians in one of the nearby Hidatsa villages with his Indian wives. He was part French and part Indian, and he often worked as an interpreter. He offered his services to Lewis and Clark and asked to join the expedition in the spring.

Charbonneau also requested permission to bring along Sacagawea, one of his Shoshone wives. [Scholars today favor Sacagawea (Sa-ka-ga-WEE-uh) over the more commonly used "Sacajawea."] Kidnapped by the Hidatsa several years ago and brought to their village, Sacagawea was no more than sixteen years old in 1804. She knew the Shoshone language and would be of great help when the expedition reached that area. Sacagawea was pregnant, but the baby was due to be born several weeks before the scheduled date of departure. The presence of a mother and baby would assure other Indian groups that the expedition was not a war party.

Lewis and Clark decided to hire Charbonneau and agreed to let him bring his

A statue of Sacagawea, the Shoshone woman who accompanied the Lewis and Clark expedition. Sacagawea proved herself to be invaluable as both a guide and interpreter.

young wife and baby along. John Bakeless says, "As they came to know Charbonneau, the captains began to realize that, whatever his shortcomings, he and Sacagawea together would be a valuable team. Charbonneau could interpret so long as they were among the river Indians; Sacagawea's knowledge of Shoshone offered their only chance of conversing with the Rocky Mountain Indians."[29]

On February 11, 1805, Sacagawea had a baby boy. He was named Jean Baptiste. In the spring, when the icy river melted and the boats started up the river once again, he would be the youngest member of the Corps of Discovery.

4 From the Mandan Villages to the Great Falls of the Missouri

Spring arrived late on the high plains, but by the last of March the river was thawing. "The ice began to brake away this evening," Clark wrote on March 25, 1805, "and was near distroying our Canoes as they wer decnding to the fort."[30]

The canoes he spoke of were six new dugouts constructed from large cottonwood trees. They replaced the keelboat, which was too large to continue up the river. Everyone was feeling good about getting under way again. "All the party in high Spirits," Clark noted. "They pass but fiew nights without amuseing themselves danceing possessing perfect harmony and good understanding towards each other."[31]

On April 3, the keelboat was packed for its return trip to St. Louis. Many "gifts" for Jefferson were boxed and placed aboard. Among them were skins and skeletons of animals such as wolf, antelope, weasel, and fox. There were horns from elk and mountain sheep. Several buffalo robes were included, one of them with a battle scene painted on it by a Mandan Indian. A Mandan bow and quiver of arrows were also among the presents, as well as a clay cooking pot made by the Indians. Plant specimens and samples of soil and minerals were enclosed.

Probably the most unusual gift for the president was a small zoo consisting of four magpies, a prairie hen, and a prairie dog. Catching the prairie dog was quite a task. These squirrel-like animals burrow in the ground, and when threatened, they dive quickly into their burrows. When efforts to capture one by digging failed, a great quantity of water was poured down one of the holes until an animal was flushed out.

Captain Lewis sent back a detailed report to Jefferson. Clark, too, dispatched letters, reports, and maps to government officials. When the keelboat left the Mandan villages on April 7, 1805, it was manned by six soldiers and nine boatmen hired for that purpose months before in St. Louis. Moses Reed, the deserter, and John Newman, who had refused to obey an order, were sent back on it also.

The expedition's "little fleet," as Lewis called it, left the same day as the keelboat, but in the opposite direction. In addition to Captains Lewis and Clark, the party consisted of three sergeants, twenty-three privates, hunter George Drouillard, York, and the Charbonneau family.

"Our vessels consisted of six small canoes, and two large perogues," Lewis wrote in his journal on April 7, 1805. "The little fleet altho' not quite so rispectable as those of Columbus or Capt. Cook, were still viewed by us with as much pleasure as

A Mandan buffalo robe which was presented to President Jefferson. The drawings on the robe depict the Mandan and their allies battling the Sioux.

those deservedly famed adventurers ever beheld theirs."[32] Lewis also remarked that this was a very happy moment for him.

In spite of all the enthusiasm, they were still rowing their boats against the current and traveling was very difficult. It was cold on the northern plains, too, with temperatures often falling below freezing. The group suffered from mosquitoes, high winds, blowing sand, smoke from prairie grass fires, and terrible odors caused by decaying buffalo which had fallen through the ice and drowned.

On the other hand, the high plains through which they were traveling swarmed with game for the hunters—buffalo, elk, deer, antelope, and beaver. During the day, Lewis walked along the shore,

examining plants, and making notes about the geography.

Even though one of their goals was to make friends with the Indians, Lewis and Clark were anxious to avoid the Assiniboine (a-SIN-a-boin) tribe, which lived along the upper Missouri River. The Assiniboine had trading ties with the Mandan and other northern tribes and did not appreciate newcomers cutting into their business. Several times they came across large abandoned campsites, but, to their relief, they never saw any people. On the other hand, they were eager to find Sacagawea's tribe, the Shoshone, who lived farther south. From them they hoped to obtain horses and information about crossing the mountains.

From the Yellowstone River to the Musselshell River

While wintering at Fort Mandan, the Hidatsa Indians had told the captains about rivers that emptied into the Missouri. As the expedition neared the place where the Yellowstone River was supposed to join the Missouri, Lewis and a small party of men set off on foot. They found the Yellowstone a few miles ahead and camped on its banks that night. The next day Clark and the rest of the crew arrived. Two days were spent there, exploring the confluence [junction] of the rivers and taking measurements.

On April 28, with favorable winds filling the sails of their boats, the explorers left the Yellowstone encampment. The high plains through which they were now traveling (northeastern Montana today) were dreary and desolate. Daily life on the expedition was anything but dreary, however. A couple of days after leaving the Yellowstone River, the party had its first encounter with grizzly bears about which the Indians had warned them. Captain Lewis wounded a grizzly bear, which chased him several yards before he killed it with a second shot. In his journal, Lewis wrote that "in the hands of a skillfull rifleman they [grizzly bears] are by no means as formidable or dangerous as they have

Expedition members encounter their first grizzly bear. Although the Indians warned them about grizzlies, they underestimated the bears' fierceness.

Those Ferocious Grizzly Bears

Captain Lewis's first encounter with a grizzly bear was not particularly frightening because the animal in question was young and much smaller than a full-grown bear. This experience led him to doubt Indian stories about how ferocious grizzlies were—but not for long! In this excerpt from Lewis and Clark: Partners in Discovery, *historian John Bakeless tells how Lewis came to change his mind.*

"They [grizzly bears] were huge brutes, often weighing up to half a ton, astonishingly fast in spite of their bulk [size], ranging in color from yellowish to very light gray, so that the expedition's journals usually refer to them as "yellow" or "white" bears. As yet unaccustomed to firearms, the grizzlies had no fear whatever of the crude one-shot rifles of the day and were extremely ferocious. . . .

No white man at that time knew much about grizzlies. In fact, except for possible trappers, traders, and hunters who left no record, no white man had ever seen them. . . . Neither Lewis nor Clark had ever seen a grizzly either, but during the long sojourn [visit] at Fort Mandan they had heard many an Indian tale about them to which they had listened with a good deal of skepticism [disbelief]. . . .

Soon after the party left the Mandan villages, grizzly tracks began to appear on the shore. . . . They were enormous. No one had ever seen anything like them. Sometimes a footprint was eleven inches long and seven and one-half inches across. But no bears were to be seen; 'the men as well as ourselves are anxious to meet with some of these bears,' wrote Lewis. . . . [He soon got his wish.] Bears now seemed to pop up all over the landscape, sometimes alone, sometimes in pairs, almost invariably [without exception] willing to stand and fight it out, or even to attack. It took the party a very short time after they reached country swarming with grizzlies to discover that the Indian hunters had been entirely correct in their accounts. . . .

Lewis revised his opinion still further: 'these bears being so hard to die [kill] reather intimedates [frightens] us all; I must confess that I do not like the gentlemen and had reather fight two Indians than one bear.'"

been represented."[33] During the next two weeks, however, Lewis completely changed his attitude about grizzly bears. Several close calls while hunting gave him a new respect for those ferocious creatures.

On May 14, 1805, some members of the expedition had another close call.

While both captains were on shore, the white pirogue was being steered by Charbonneau, who could not swim. A sudden wind caught the sail of the pirogue and spun it around, causing Charbonneau to panic. Pierre Cruzatte, also aboard, managed to keep the craft from sinking. Another passenger, Sacagawea, rescued most of the important objects and papers that spilled out.

Watching from the shore, Lewis was horrified. According to his own account, "I for a moment forgot my own situation, and involluntarily droped my gun, threw aside my shot pouch and was in the act of unbuttoning my coat, before I recollected the folly of the attempt I was about to make; which was to throw myself into the river and indevour to swim to the perogue."[34]

Fortunately, Cruzatte and others got the pirogue safely ashore. An inventory of the contents showed that nothing of major importance had been lost. Lewis gave credit to Sacagawea for her quick action: "the Indian woman to whom I ascribe equal fortitude and resolution, with any person onboard at the time of the accedent," he wrote in his journal, "caught and preserved most of the light articles which were washed overboard."[35]

Moving West from the Musselshell River

On May 20, 1805, the expedition reached the mouth of the Musselshell River. There they camped while Lewis and Clark took measurements and the hunters went out to bring in fresh game.

One day the hunters found a pretty little river running into the Musselshell.

"The hunters returned this evening," Lewis wrote, "and informed us that . . . about five miles abe (above) the mouth of shell [Musselshell] river a handsome river of about fifty yards in width discharged itself into the shell river . . . [and] this stream we call Sah-ca-ger we-ah or bird woman's River, after our interpreter the Snake [Shoshone] woman."[36]

Gradually, the Missouri River was becoming more shallow and harder to navigate. It often became necessary to tow the boats from the banks as well as row them. This duty was extremely hard on the men's feet because the banks were covered with sharp stones and prickly pear cactus. Their shoes had long since worn out, and moccasins afforded very little protection against these annoyances. The men also suffered from various ailments caused by spending so much time in cold, muddy water.

But the hunting was still good, and a new item was added to the menu—Rocky Mountain bighorn sheep. On May 25, 1805, three were killed. Lewis examined them carefully and wrote a detailed description of the species in his journal.

A few nights later, the party barely escaped destruction from an animal of another species. A large buffalo bull swam across the river, clambered over the white pirogue, and charged into the camp. Before the soldier on guard duty could head him off, he galloped through the encampment, barely missing the sleeping men. He then ran headlong toward the lodge where the captains were sleeping, but "when he came near the tent," Lewis wrote later, "my dog saved us by causing him to change his course a second time, which he did by turning a little to the right, and was quickly out of sight. . . . we were happy to find no one hirt."[37]

Still moving west, the boats were now passing through a canyon with strange rock formations (today called the Missouri Breaks). Lewis described this fascinating area in his journal on May 31, 1805:

The hills and river Clifts which we passed today exhibit a most romantic [mysterious] appearance. The bluffs on the river rise to the hight of from 2 to 300 feet and in most places nearly perpendicular [straight up]; they are formed of remarkable white sandstone. . . . The water in the course of time in decending from those hills and plains on either side of the river has trickled down the soft sand clifts and woarn it into a thousand grotesque figures, which with the help of a little imagination . . . are made to represent eligant ranges of lofty freestone buildings. . . . so perfect indeed are those walls that I should have thought that nature had attempted here to rival the human art of masonry.[38]

The Big Question: Which River Is the Missouri?

On Sunday, June 2, 1805, the expedition was faced unexpectedly with a serious problem. The information given to them by the Hidatsa had been reasonably accurate most of the way. Suddenly, however, the Missouri River forked, one stream turning southwest and the other continuing in a northwesterly direction. Either the Indians had not mentioned this junction or the captains had misunderstood the information they'd received. Since both forks were about the same size, the leaders were at a loss to know which fork

was the Missouri. Lewis expressed the seriousness of the problem this way:

To mistake the stream at this period of the season, two months of the traveling season having now elapsed, and to ascend such stream to the rocky Mountain or perhaps much further before we could inform ourselves whether it did approach the Columbia [a river that was known to flow into the Pacific Ocean] or not, and then be obliged to return and take the other stream would not only loose us the whole of this season but would probably so dishearten the party that it might defeat the expedition altogether.[39]

The crew members argued that the north fork was the Missouri because, for one thing, it was going in the right direction. It was muddy, too, just like the river on which they had traveled for hundreds of miles. The south fork, on the other hand, was almost clear and heading in the wrong direction.

The captains, however, believed that the south fork was the Missouri. The Hidatsa had told them that the Missouri River ran almost north for a time near its headwaters. Then it roared over some tremendous falls before it turned back east. If they were getting close to the headwaters (and Lewis and Clark believed they were), the water coming from the mountains should be clear rather than muddy.

In spite of the captains' logic, the men were not convinced. Not wishing to destroy the high morale the crew had shown throughout the difficult journey, the captains compromised. They agreed to send out a small party to explore each fork for a day and a half's march. Upon the return of these groups, a final decision would be

This fanciful painting depicts the Lewis and Clark expedition high atop the bluffs on the Missouri River. These steep cliffs were a source of fascination for the expedition members.

made. On June 4, 1805, both parties left camp. Clark's group followed the south fork and Lewis's group headed up the north fork.

Clark's exploring trip was relatively uneventful, but Captain Lewis and one of his men nearly met disaster. Rain had turned the river banks into slippery mud. Lewis slipped and very nearly plunged over a cliff. He saved himself by digging his espontoon (a short spear or lance) into the ground. Seconds later, Private Windsor also slipped, but managed to cling to the edge of the cliff. Speaking calmly, Lewis told him what to do, and Windsor dragged himself up the bank to safety.

After exploring the north fork for several miles, Lewis was convinced it was not the Missouri. He named it Maria's River in honor of a distant cousin in Virginia whom he admired. Only a few days before, Clark had named the Judith River for Julia Hancock, the young lady who would later become his wife. (Clark had only known Julia a short time and was mistaken about her first name.)

Finding the Great Falls

Clark's party returned first. Two days later, Lewis's group arrived. Sergeant Ordway recorded both events in his journal:

June 6th Thursday 1805 . . . about 2 oClock P.M. Capt. Clark and his party returned to Camp

had been about 40 miles up the South fork & Capt Clark thinks it will be the best course for us to go. . . . Saturday 8th June 1805. . . . about 3 oClock P.M. Capt Lewis & his party returned to Camp, & Informed us that they had walked through high plains for about 60 miles up the north fork. . . . Capt Lewis thinks that the N. fork bears too far north for our course. . . . so our Captains conclude to assend the South fork and burry some articles which we can do without & leave the largest perogue.[40]

Now that it had been decided to follow the south fork, a plan was set in motion. Lewis and a small party would go ahead to look for the falls the Indians had told them about. Clark would break camp and follow as soon as possible.

Lewis left on June 11, 1805. Two days later, he and his party heard the sound of roaring water ahead of them. A short time later, they reached the falls. They were elated. Now they knew for certain that the south fork was the Missouri. Lewis described the magnificent scene in his journal, calling it "the grandest sight I ever beheld."[41]

The next day, Lewis sent Joseph Field back to tell Clark they had found the falls. While looking for a portage [dry passage] around the big drop, Lewis discovered

that there were five falls of varying sizes and shapes in a ten-mile stretch of the river. As beautiful as the falls were, they also meant hard times ahead. The boats and supplies would have to be carried around them for many miles.

Back at the camp, Captain Clark and the rest of the group were preparing to follow. They cached [hid] a number of nonessential articles by burying them in a pit. The red pirogue was hidden in the brush along the river. With a lighter burden, the main party moved up the river a day behind Lewis.

Sacagawea played little or no part in the decisions about which fork to take, being no more familiar with this area than anyone else. Her girlhood home was still far to the south. Besides, the diaries tell us that she was very ill at this time. So ill, in fact, that the captains feared for her life. Even when traveling, she lay feverish and listless in the pirogue.

On June 16, when Lewis rejoined the main group, he was much alarmed at Sacagawea's condition. Although Captain Clark had done everything for her that he could, Lewis decided to try another remedy. He persuaded her to drink some water from a sulfur spring he had discovered. The very next day he reported, "The Indian woman much better today. . . . she is free from pain [and] clear of fever, her pulse regular, and eats as heartily as I am willing to permit her of broiled buffaloe well seasoned with pepper and salt and rich soope of the same meat; I think therefore that there is every rational hope of her recovery."[42]

Whether the captains' remedies did the trick, or whether Sacagawea's youth and strength pulled her through, no one can say. She was soon her old self again,

Flash Flood at the Great Falls

On June 29, 1805, it was too wet to move baggage, so Clark decided to take another look at the falls. York and the Charbonneau family went along. The outing almost ended in disaster when a sudden storm broke over the river. Captain Clark recorded the incident in his diary. These excerpts are taken from The Journals of Lewis and Clark, *edited by Bernard DeVoto.*

"I deturmined my self to proceed to the falls . . . according[ly] we all set out, I took my servant & one man, Chabono [Charbonneau] our Interpreter & his Squar [squaw—Sacagawea] accompanied, soon after I arrived at the falls, I perceived a cloud which appeared black and threaten imediate rain, I looked out for a shelter but could see no place without being in great danger of being blown into the river if the wind should prove as turbelant as it is at some times about ¼ of a mile above the falls I obsd [observed] a Deep riveen [ravine] in which was shelveing rocks under which we took shelter. . . . soon after a torrent of rain and hail fell more violent than ever I saw before, the rain fell like one voley of water falling from the heavens and gave us time only to get out of the way of a torrent of water which was Poreing down the hill in the River with emence force tareing everything before it takeing with it large rocks & mud, I took my gun and shot pouch in my left hand, and with the right scrambled up the hill pushing the Interpreters wife (who had her child in her arms) before me, the Interpreter himself makeing attempts to pull his wife up by the hand much scared and nearly without motion, we at length reached the top of the hill safe where I found my servent in serch of us greatly agitated, for our wellfar. before I got out of the bottom of the raveen . . . the water was up to my waste. . . . I scercely got out before it raised 10 feet with a torrent which [was] turrouble to behold, and by the time I reached the top of the hill, at least 15 feet water, I derected the party to return to camp . . . where Clothes could be got to cover the child whose clothes were all lost, and the woman who was but just recovering from a severe indisposition [illness], and was wet and cold. . . . I caused her as also the others of the party to take a little spirits . . . which revived [them] verry much."

ready to help with one of the hardest tasks to face the Corps of Discovery so far—making a portage around the Great Falls of the Missouri River.

The Portage Around the Great Falls

By June 17, the expedition had moved as close to the falls as they could get. They decided to make their portage on the south side of the river, and a base camp was established at a nearby creek. Taking a few men with him, Captain Clark left to take measurements of the falls, and to find the best route around them. The first task was relatively easy. David Lavender reports, "The full stretch of cascades and rapids came to . . . 14.8 miles. In that distance, Clark computed, the Missouri dropped 360 feet and two inches. The first and biggest waterfall was 87 feet and 3/4 inch high; the next tallest . . . turned out to be 47 feet 8 inches."[43]

Finding a way around the falls was more difficult, but Clark and his men managed to stake out a rough trail for the company to follow. They also established another base camp eighteen and one-quarter miles away from the first. On June 20, 1805, they returned to the first camp.

Lewis and the rest of the company had been very busy in their absence. They had built two crude wagons with wheels cut from cottonwood trees. For axles they used the mast from the white pirogue (that vessel being too large to portag. The men also spent time reinforcing the moccasins with rawhide to help protect their feet from prickly pear cactus.

On June 13, 1805, Lewis and his party sighted the Great Falls of the Missouri River.

On June 22, the actual portage began. Historian David Hawke describes it this way:

The two rickety wagons carried all their brittle wheels and spindly axletrees could bear. Progress was torturous. Prickly pears abounded everywhere and no one could avoid their spines. Herds of buffalo had trod the turf into a hard, knobby carpet. . . . The heaviest burden fell on those who

EXPERIMENT, The Iron Boat

Before the expedition began, Meriwether Lewis designed a collapsible boat frame, to be assembled and covered with birch bark or hides when needed. He named it Experiment. *The frame was carried all the way past the Great Falls, where Lewis determined to put it to use. Historian David Freeman Hawke discusses the results in this excerpt from* Those Tremendous Mountains: The Story of the Lewis and Clark Expedition.

"July 4 saw the boat sheathed [covered with buffalo and elk skins]. It was submerged in the river to shrink the skins tight, then placed on a rack above small fires to dry her. His dream boat's appearance pleased Lewis immensely. . . . 'She is strong and will carry at least eight thousand pounds. . . . Her form is as complete as I could wish it.' He knew the most difficult job lay ahead—'that of making her seams secure. . . .'

The next day nearly broke Lewis' heart. He awoke to see stitch holes gaping where the skins had dried tight against the boat frame. [Lewis filled the holes with a caulk made from ground charcoal, beeswax, and buffalo tallow.] They launched the *Experiment* . . . on July 9. 'She lay like a perfect cork on the water.' Lewis ordered seats installed and oars fitted. . . . Then without warning a violent wind churned the river into crashing waves. . . . When it subsided the iron boat lay up to her gunwales [sides] in water. . . . Much of the composition [caulk] had peeled away 'and left the seams of the boat exposed to the water and she leaked in such manner that she would not answer [be fit to use].' . . . Lewis ordered the boat sunk until the skins had become soft enough to retrieve. [The frame was then buried.] Lewis remarked 'that this circumstance mortified [embarrassed] me not a little,' and thereafter said no more about his boat. He and Clark, indeed, all in the party, excelled at putting the past behind and moving on to whatever pain or pleasure the future held."

pulled the wagons in harnesses made of elk hide. . . . Sweat poured off every man. . . . They made eight miles by noontime. Darkness caught them still some distance from the campsite at the head of the falls. They pushed on until the tongue of one wagon gave way. Every man loaded up with all the baggage he could manage and trudged on. . . . They reached camp to find wolves had eaten most of the meat Clark had left there. . . . The next morning the men backpacked in the luggage left behind the night before and then departed for the lower camp trundling the empty wagons.[44]

For days the men struggled with their burdens from the lower to the upper camp, but the hard work of portaging was only one of their problems. One day, a sudden storm struck with hail so big it bruised the men and even knocked them off their feet. Grizzly bears constantly harassed them at the upper camp, and a flash flood almost drowned Clark, York, and the Charbonneau family.

To lighten their burden, they decided to cache a lot more of their goods, even leaving behind barrels of flour and pork. By early July, all their baggage finally was assembled at the upper base camp. Everyone was eager to be off, but another unexpected delay occurred.

For hundreds of miles, the party had transported Lewis's collapsible boat frame, *Experiment*. Now that the white pirogue had to be left behind, Lewis decided it was time to put his boat together. He sewed a covering of elk and buffalo hides, but the caulking material he made to seal the seams wouldn't stick. To add to the problem, a sudden storm hit and filled the vessel with water. The *Experiment* had to be abandoned. It was then necessary to construct two new dugout canoes to take its place.

On July 15, 1805, all was ready at last. The fleet of eight dugout canoes, minus a lot of baggage and the collapsible boat frame, pushed up the Missouri once more. It was good to be sailing on smooth water again, but the joy didn't last long. Ahead of them the party could see another surprise: high cliffs rising above the river on both sides. The boats were about to enter a deep gorge.

5 From the Great Falls of the Missouri to the Lolo Trail

As the expedition moved upstream, open banks still lay along the river where men could walk and hunt. Ahead, however, the mountains came right down to the river. Lewis and three men advanced on foot. After taking latitude readings, they hiked five miles into the river canyon, about forty miles north of present-day Helena, Montana. There they waited for the boats.

After catching up with Lewis, Clark left the river with a small party to hunt and look for the Shoshone people. The going was very rough. The cliffs above the river were steep, and the rocks and prickly pear cactus injured their feet badly. Game was scarce, and the men began to feel hunger for the first time.

Meanwhile, Lewis stayed on the river with the boats. It was hard going there, too, since now that the river filled the entire channel, there was no place to camp or hunt. On July 19, Lewis wrote:

this evening we entered much the most remarkable clifts we have yet seen. these clifts rise from the waters edge on either side perpendicularly [straight up] to the hight of (about) 1200 feet. every object here wears a dark and gloomy aspect. the tow[er]ing and projecting rocks in many places seem ready to tumble on us. . . . the river ap-

pears to have woarn a passage just the width of its channel or 150 yds. it is deep from side to side nor is ther in the 1st 3 Miles of this distance a spot except one of a few yards in extent on which a man could rest the soal of his foot. . . . from the singular [unusual] appearance of this place I called it the *gates of the rocky mountains.*[45]

By July 22, the river party had emerged from the canyon, tired and weary. Sacagawea cheered them up by recognizing the country through which they were now traveling. She assured them that the headwaters of the Missouri lay just ahead, where the river forked into three streams. Captain Lewis remarked, "this piece of information has cheered the sperits of the party who now begin to console [comfort] themselves with the anticipation of shortly seeing the head of the missouri yet unknown to the civilized world."[46]

The Three Forks of the Missouri River

Captain Clark rejoined the boats briefly, but left again early the next day to continue searching for the Shoshone. There

Sacagawea reassures Lewis and Clark (center) that they are near the headwaters of the Missouri River.

were signs all around that people had camped in the area, but not one could be found. On July 25, 1805, Clark and his advance party reached the point at which the Missouri River divides into three forks. Leaving a note tied to a pole where Lewis would be sure to find it, they went off to explore the area. Two days later, when Lewis and the boats arrived at the Three Forks, Lewis wrote:

> the country opens suddonly to extensive and beatifull plains and meadows which appear to be surrounded in every direction with distant and lofty mountains; supposing this to be the three forks of the Missouri I halted the party. . . . and ascended the point of a high limestone clift from whence I commanded a most perfect view of the neighbouring country.[47]

Later in the day, Captain Clark and his party returned to the camp, ill and exhausted from their recent marches. To give everyone a much-needed rest, the captains decided to stay put for a few days. While at the Three Forks, they named the rivers. As Lewis reported it:

> [W]e called the S.W. fork, that which we meant to ascend, Jefferson's River in honor of that illustrious [outstanding] personage Thomas Jefferson. . . . the Middle fork we called Madison's River in honor of James Madison [secretary of state], and the S.E. Fork we called Gallitin's River in honor of Albert Gallitin [secretary of the treasury].[48]

On July 30, they broke camp and began following the river they had named for Jefferson. It was a matter of great

The Rocky Mountains

In the early nineteenth century, no one had a clear idea of the geography of western North America. Lewis and Clark probably knew more than most, but even they were surprised by the Rocky Mountains. In this excerpt from Passage Through the Garden: Lewis and Clark and the Image of the American Northwest, *geographer John Logan Allen compares Lewis and Clark's image of the Rocky Mountains with what they actually found.*

"The Corps of Discovery had reached the Rocky Mountains and for the next three months would endeavor to untangle the mazes of those massive ranges, so different from all other mountains within the framework of early nineteenth-century American environmental experience and imagination. The wide and beautiful plains were no more, and Lewis and Clark and their command [soldiers] would struggle through nearly impossible terrain until they reached the Pacific slopes and the navigable waters of the Columbia [River] system. In their search for the passage through the Rockies, Lewis and Clark would come to realize more and more the discrepancy [difference] between the image [mental picture] with which they had left Fort Mandan and the actuality of western geography. . . .

By the evening of July 21, the expedition had passed the worst stretch of the canyon of the Missouri and the valley again widened, although not, as Lewis and Clark might have expected, into a broad and flat intermountain region like the Shenandoah valley [on the east coast]. The river was still surrounded by mountains of astonishing height, with characteristics that were difficult to comprehend. . . . They were nothing like any mountains the American explorers had ever seen. . . . And the farther the explorers penetrated into the mountainous country, the more awesome the mighty ranges became, [Clark wrote] 'one range above another as they recede from the river untill the most distant and lofty have their tops clad with snow. the adjacent mountains commonly rise so high as to conceal the more distant and lofty mountains from our view.'"

concern that they still had seen no Indians. To cross the mountains, they needed horses, and they had no possible source other than the Shoshone.

Sacagawea continued to reassure the men. Her people had to be nearby, she told them. She had often visited the area as a child and in fact had been kidnapped from this very place by the Hidatsa. Private Joseph Whitehouse made note of that fact. In his diary dated July 30, 1805, he wrote:

> a clear pleasant morning. we loaded the canoes eairly and Set out about 9 oClock and proceeded on. . . . Capt. Lewis and Several men walked on Shore. . . . we passed large bottoms of cotton timber. the River crooked rapid and full of Islands, the underbrushes thick. the currents [currants, a type of berry] abound. the beaver pleanty. . . . at this place our Intrepters wife [Sacagawea] was taken prisoner 4 years ago by a war party of the [Hidatsa]. they took hir as She was attempting to make hir ascape by crossing a Shole place [shoal or shallow place] on the River, but was taken in the middle of it. 2 or 3 Indians killed at the Same time on Shore. the rest of the Snakes [Shoshones] made their ascape.[49]

On August 1, the two captains separated again. This time Lewis took an advance party to explore the upper reaches of the Jefferson River and to renew the search for the Shoshone. Clark and the rest of the company stayed on the river with the canoes. As they moved closer to the mountains, the river became more and more shallow, twisting, and difficult to navigate. On August 6, the two groups met again briefly, but neither had seen any Indians.

A couple of days later, Sacagawea recognized a high cliff which the Indians called the beaver's head. Nearby, she told them, was a pass where her people crossed the mountains to hunt. Determined to find the pass, Lewis set out the next day with Drouillard and two other men. Before leaving, he wrote:

> [Sacagawea] assures us that we shall either find her people on this river or on the river immediately west of it's source. . . . as it is now all important with us to meet with those people as soon as possible I determined . . . to proceed tomorrow with a small party. . . . in short it is my resolution to find them or some others, who have

Sacagawea guides the Corps of Discovery through her Shoshone homeland.

horses if it should cause me a trip of one month. for without horses we shall be obliged to leave a great part of our stores.[50]

Lewis Meets the Shoshone

Lewis and his men located the pass (called the Lemhi Pass today), and on August 10, they crossed the continental divide, where the rivers drain to the Pacific Ocean. The next day, they spied a Shoshone man on horseback, but he rode quickly away. Two days later, Lewis came upon an old Shoshone woman and two young girls. At first they were terrified, but when Lewis gave them presents, they agreed to take him to their village.

As they walked toward the village, sixty Shoshone warriors on horseback came riding full speed toward them. The chief, Cameahwait [ca-ME-uh-wait], was in the lead. Lewis quickly put his gun aside and grabbed the American flag. He wrote later that

> when they arrived I advanced towards them with the flag leaving my gun with the party about 50 paces behind me. the chief and two others who were a little in advance of the main body spoke to the women, and they informed them who we were and exultingly [happily] shewed the presents which had been given them these men then advanced and embraced me very affectionately.[51]

Lewis and his men accompanied the Shoshone to their village where they remained for the next few days. The Indians were preparing for a buffalo hunt, a risky undertaking. Not only was the hunt dangerous, but going out on the plains exposed them to their well-armed enemies. With only a few guns, the Shoshone were no match for the Hidatsa. There was "nothing to be seen among . . . them," Sergeant Ordway noted in his diary, "but their horses & 2 or 3 guns, but no ammunition. . . . they have no knives tommahawks nor no weapons of war except their bow & arrows."[52] Nevertheless, hunger compelled them to risk a buffalo hunt on the open prairie once in a while.

With Drouillard translating by means of sign language, Lewis told Chief Cameahwait about the great father in Washington who wanted to bring trade goods to the Indians in exchange for furs. Perhaps the Shoshone could even get the guns they needed so badly. To bring this all about, Lewis said, he needed horses for himself and for the other members of his company who were waiting just across the divide with presents for the Indians. There was even a young Shoshone woman with them. Would Cameahwait and his people go with him to meet his party and bring back the gifts?

Cameahwait hesitated. He liked the white men, but he wasn't sure how far to trust them. Maybe they were leading him into a trap. Growing impatient, Lewis hinted that perhaps Cameahwait and his warriors were *afraid* to go. Cameahwait hotly denied the charge. To prove they were not cowards, he said they would go with him.

On August 15, the combined parties began trekking toward the divide to meet Captain Clark and the rest of the Corps. Everyone was hungry, and Lewis sent his men out to hunt. When Drouillard killed a deer and began to cut it open, the Indians ran to it and quickly devoured the uncooked entrails [guts] on the spot. Lewis was shocked. "I viewed these poor starved divils with pity and compassion," he wrote. "I directed McNeal to skin the deer and reserved a quarter, the ballance I gave the Chief to be divided among his people; they devoured the whole of it nearly without cooking."[53]

As the travelers continued toward the divide, Lewis became extremely uneasy. What if Clark were not there? Chief Cameahwait and his people were anxious, too. What if this were an ambush? It was a

Indian Sign Language

Although the American Indians had many spoken languages, they also communicated effectively with one another silently, through signs. On several occasions, the captains made good use of this practical form of communication. These excerpts are from The Journals of Lewis and Clark, *edited by Bernard DeVoto, and* Original Journals of the Lewis and Clark Expedition, *edited by Reuben Gold Thwaites.*

"[At the Shoshone camp, August 14, 1805] The means I had of communicating with these people was by way of Drewyer [Drouillard] who understood perfectly the common language of jesticulation [gestures] or signs which seem to be universally understood by all the Nations we have yet seen. it is true that this language is imperfect and liable to error but it is much less so than would be expected. the strong parts of the ideas are seldom mistaken."

"[Meeting with three Flatheads on September 10, 1805] Our guide could not speake the language of these people but soon engaged them in conversation by signs or gesticulation, the common language of all the Aborigines [natives] of North America, it is one understood by all of them and appears to be sufficiently copious [expressive] to convey with a degree of certainty the outlines of what they wish to communicate."

"[Meetings with Twisted Hair, Nez Percé chief, September 22 and 23, 1805] . . . we attempted to have some talk with those people but could not for the want of an Interpreter thro' which we could Speake, [and] we were compelled to converse altogether by Signs. . . . We assembled the principal Men as well as the Chiefs and by Signs informed them where we came from [and of] our wish to inculcate [create] peace and good understanding between all the red people &c. which appeared to Satisfy them much."

Indians engage in a buffalo hunt. During such events the Indians not only risked injury from the powerful prey, they also chanced being attacked by their enemies while on the open prairie.

tense group that arrived at the meeting place on August 16, 1805. It soon became even more tense, because Clark was *not* there. A note Lewis had left for him was untouched.

At first, Lewis did not know what to do. Then he got an idea. He pretended the note was *from* Clark, saying that Clark and the rest of the party were camping close by. The Indians were suspicious, but they agreed to wait until the next day. After a sleepless night, Lewis sent out Drouillard early the next morning to find Clark and tell him to get there as fast as he could.

Fortunately, Clark was already on the way, and within two hours, he and the rest of the party reached the encampment. Clark wrote on August 17, 1805:

We Set out at 7 oClock and proceeded on to the forks [a place on the Jefferson River where a creek entered] I had not proceeded on one mile before I saw at a distance Several Indians on horseback Comeing towards me, The Intertrepeter & Squar [Sacagawea] who were before me at Some distance danced for the joyful Sight, and She made signs to me that they were her nation. . . . those Indians Sung all the way to their Camp.[54]

While Sacagawea was joyfully reuniting with friends and relatives who had never expected to see her again, Clark went on, and was received by Captain Lewis and Chief Cameahwait. The chief welcomed

Captain Clark with solemn ceremonies and the smoking of the pipe.

With Sacagawea's help, the captains hoped to be able to explain their mission more fully. However, since Sacagawea did not speak English, they had to set up an interpretation chain. One of the captains gave a message in English to Francis Labiche, a Corps member who spoke both English and French. Labiche translated it into French for Charbonneau. Charbonneau translated the message into Hidatsa for Sacagawea. She, in turn, translated it into Shoshone for the chief!

It was during this transaction that another stirring moment occurred. "As the talks began," David Lavender writes, "recognition came to her again, this time like a blow. The chief was her brother! Inexpressibly agitated [flustered], she threw her blanket over his head (a sign, perhaps, of their sibling bond) and burst into tears. After the two had wept together for a time, the ceremony resumed."[55]

The Captains Make a New Plan

In following the Missouri River to its source, the expedition had moved far south of where it needed to be to reach the Columbia River, the known route to the Pacific. It would now be necessary to turn back north, either on an overland trail or by another river that might connect with the Columbia.

Together, the captains decided upon a plan. Clark would take several of the men and look for a navigable river on the other side of the divide. If they didn't find one, they would scout out the best overland route to take. While Clark was gone, Lewis, with the help of the Indians, would move the baggage to the village.

The next day, August 18, Lewis traded some of the expedition's goods for three horses: two for Captain Clark's journey and one for the hunters who would stay with

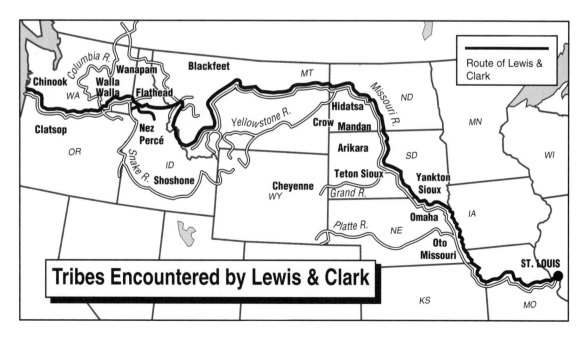

Tribes Encountered by Lewis & Clark

him. At ten o'clock, Chief Cameahwait and most of the Indians set out for the Shoshone village along with Captain Clark, eleven of his men, and the Charbonneau family. They arrived two days later. After urging the Indians to hurry back to help Captain Lewis, Clark and his party departed on their exploratory mission.

In the meantime, Lewis and his men were busy at the expedition camp making pack saddles and caching more of the things they couldn't take with them. On August 22, Cameahwait and a large party of Shoshone returned from the village with horses, as they had promised. Lewis prepared a meal of boiled corn and beans for them, which they enjoyed very much. Later that evening, he directed the building of a fish trap whereby they caught over five hundred trout.

On August 24, they finally started transporting the baggage to the village. On the way, Lewis was able to trade for several more horses and a mule. All seemed to be going well when Lewis learned that the Indians secretly planned to meet other Shoshone coming from their village, and then go off on the buffalo hunt immediately. Lewis was upset by this news because without assistance from the Indians, the expedition would never get the horses it needed. He immediately confronted Chief Cameahwait, and after more persuasion and some tough talk, the chief agreed to continue the march to the village. On August 26, 1805, more than two weeks after Lewis had first encountered the Shoshone, they arrived at the village with the baggage.

Corps member John Colter was waiting there with a message from Captain Clark. No navigable river could be found, the note said. The next part of the jour-

ney would have to be made on foot, and the going would be rough. Sergeant Gass, who was with Clark, described some of the obstacles the men encountered across the divide. "We proceeded down the river through dreadful narrows," he wrote, "where the rocks were in some places breast high, and no path or trail of any kind."[56]

Lewis knew for certain now that they would have to have many more horses. "[I] therefore determined to commence the purchase of horses in the morning from the indians," Lewis wrote, "in order to carry into execution the design we had formed of passing the rocky Mountains."[57]

Trading for horses with the Shoshone was not an easy task. Horses were their

Despite setbacks, Lewis remained eager to finalize the trading with the Shoshone and continue exploring the vast, unknown territory.

Hardships of the Shoshone Life

Spanish traders sold horses but not guns to the Shoshone. The Shoshone's enemies, however, had both horses and guns, which they obtained from traders in their own areas. This inequality caused great suffering for the Shoshone, as Captain Lewis recorded in his journal on August 20, 1805. The excerpt is from The Journals of the Lewis and Clark Expedition, *edited by Gary E. Moulton.*

"I can discover that these people are by no means friendly to the Spaniards their complaint is, that the Spaniards will not let them have fire arms and ammunition, that they put them off by telling them that if they suffer [allow] them to have guns they will kill each other, thus leaving them defenceless and an easy prey to their bloodthirsty neighbors to the East of them, who being in possession of fire arms hunt them up and murder them without rispect to sex or age and plunder them of their horses on all occasions. they told me that to avoid their enemies who were eternally harrassing them that they were obliged to remain in the interior of these mountains at least two thirds of the year where they suffered . . . . great heardships for the want of food sometimes living for weeks without meat and only a little fish roots and berries. but this added Cameahwait, with his ferce eyes and lank jaws grown meager [thin] for the want of food, would not be the case if we had guns, we could then live in the country of buffaloe and eat as our enimies do and not be compelled to hide ourselves in these mountains and live on roots and berries as the bear do. we do not fear our enimies when placed on an equal footing with them."

only form of wealth, and besides, they needed mounts and pack animals for the upcoming buffalo hunt. By the time Lewis and Clark left the Shoshone village on August 30, 1805, they had been able to obtain only twenty-eight horses and a mule, and the expedition had paid dearly for the beasts in trade goods.

The departing company consisted of thirty-nine people—two captains, twenty-six soldiers, York, Drouillard, the Charbonneau family, Toby (an Indian guide), his son, and four young Shoshone men (who turned back a few days later). Seaman, Lewis's dog, was still with them.

On the Trail in the Bitterroot Mountains

.

Toby had warned that the trail was rough, and it soon became clear how right he was. As the party made their way over fallen timbers, through dense underbrush, and across rock-strewn slopes, it sometimes seemed as if there were no trail at all. Game was scarce, and the nights were cold. Many times a pack horse slipped and rolled down the sides of the steep trail. Before the unfortunate animal could struggle to its feet, it had to be unloaded and led back up the slope.

There was one stroke of good luck, however. Dropping down into a meadow one day, they came upon a camp of friendly members of the Flathead tribe who were on their way to hunt buffalo. The Flathead language and their character impressed the expedition members. Private Whitehouse wrote about the Flatheads in his journal. "These Savages has the Strangest language of any we have ever Seen," he said. "They appear to us to have an Empediment [flaw] in their Speech or a brogue or bur on their tongue but they are the likelyest and honestst Savages we have ever yet Seen."[58]

The Flatheads proved to be generous as well: "in the Course of the day," Clark wrote, "I purchased 11 horses & exchanged 7 for which we gave a fiew articles of merchandise, those people possess ellegant horses."[59]

On September 6, the Corps moved on. With about forty good horses in hand, they felt encouraged as they moved through the beautiful Bitterroot Valley in present-day Montana. With Toby as their guide, they were looking for an Indian trail that would lead them across the mountains toward the Columbia River. A few more days of traveling brought them to a place beside a creek they called Traveller's Rest, and that is what they did. After two days, they moved on again.

Shortly afterward, they found what they were looking for—the trail across the

Expedition members were greatly impressed by the Flathead tribe's generosity and affability.

mountains used by the Nez Percé on their way to hunt buffalo. Toby informed them that a four-day journey east on this trail would take them directly to the Missouri River, not far from the place Lewis had named the Gates of the Mountains! The route followed by the Corps of Discovery from that place had taken nearly two months of hard traveling. They had no regrets, however. Their mission was to explore the Missouri River to its headwaters and that is what they had done.

On September 11, 1805, the expedition members turned their faces westward. They were now on an Indian trail that would later be called the Lolo Trail. Although they didn't know it at the time, the Lolo Trail was to test their courage and endurance as nothing else had done on this long and dangerous journey.

6 From the Lolo Trail to the Pacific Ocean

Even though it was early in September, frost covered the ground over which the expedition traveled. More worrisome than the frost was the sight of the snow-covered mountain peaks ahead, as far as the eye could see. On September 13, Lewis and Clark came upon a pleasant place where hot springs bubbled out of the mountainside. The Indians had created a bathing pool there, but the party didn't linger. They had a long way to go, and traveling conditions were becoming more difficult with each mile.

Not far from the hot springs, they crossed a high mountain pass and dropped into a valley where the land was very rugged. Working their way along the banks of a swift river, the hunters could find no game. They were forced to kill and eat one of the colts they had obtained from the Flatheads. They also began eating the portable soup Lewis had bought in Philadelphia. They didn't like it, but it kept them alive.

After struggling along the river for a day, Toby, the Shoshone guide, began to realize that he had made a serious mistake. The trail they were following was not the main trail, but a fishing path occasionally used by the Nez Percé. The main trail was on top of the ridge. On September 15, they were forced to climb four thousand

feet to reach the main trail. It was a terrible climb. Captain Clark described it in his journal:

This drawing of the Lolo Trail was taken from one of Clark's journals. During the extensive expedition, Clark was the primary mapmaker.

the road leaves the river to the left and assends a *mountain* winding in every direction to get up the Steep assents & to pass the emence [immense] quantity of falling timber. . . . Several horses Sliped and roled down Steep hills which hurt them verry much the one which Carried my desk & Small trunk Turned over & roled down a mountain for 40 yards & lodged against a tree, broke the Desk the horse escaped and appeared but little hurt. . . . after two hours delay we proceeded on up the mountain Steep & ruged as usial.[60]

They finally reached the main trail, and "when we awoke this morning," Private Whitehouse wrote in his diary on September 16, "to our great Surprise we were covred with Snow which had fallen about 2 Inches the latter part of last night, and continues a verry cold Snow Storm. . . . could hardly See the old trail for the Snow. . . . the Snow is fell So fast that it is now in common 5 or 6 Inches deep."[61]

Clumps of heavy snow dropped on them from tree branches as they passed underneath, soaking them to the skin. Almost in despair, Clark wrote, "I have been wet and as cold in every part as I ever was in my life, indeed I was at one time fearfull my feet would freeze in the thin mockersons which I wore."[62]

That evening, they killed another colt, ate half of it, and saved the rest for breakfast. On September 18, desperate for food, Clark and a small group of men went ahead to find game. From a high peak, they saw a prairie about forty miles ahead where the mountains ended. They were heartened by the sight, but they had a long way to go, and they were very, very

Much of our knowledge of the expedition is derived from the diaries kept by the Corps members. This detailed drawing was found in Clark's journal.

hungry. Coming upon a stray Indian horse, they killed it for food. They cooked part of it and left the rest hanging in a tree for Lewis's party.

Two days later Clark and his men emerged from the mountains at a place now known as the Weippe (WEE-ipe) Prairie. A group of friendly Nez Percé camping nearby gave them dried salmon and bread made from camas bulbs, a kind of lily that grows in the meadows. The advance party moved on to a second village and were welcomed there also. That evening, Clark and his men became very

Captain Clark, Cartographer

Although William Clark had no formal training, he was the expedition's main cartographer (mapmaker). Achieved with only a few measuring instruments and with his own sharp powers of observation, his maps were amazingly accurate. This tribute to Clark's skill is from Atlas of the Lewis and Clark Expedition, *edited by Gary E. Moulton.*

"It is now widely known that Clark was the principal mapmaker for the expedition. He is the author, direct or indirect, of all but a few of the 129 historic maps in this volume [the Atlas]. Lewis, the expedition's naturalist, seems to have drafted none of the maps presented here. Moreover, of the nearly 60 maps set down in the journals, only 2 can be attributed to Lewis. If Clark's productive capacity seems incredible for a man charged with numerous administrative and routine duties, one is equally amazed at his drafting [mechanical drawing] capabilities. Working with crude and unreliable instruments and with no apparent training in cartography, Clark did a masterful job, and his drafting abilities have been universally admired. . . .

Clark's mapping of the West accomplished the expedition's principal objective—to explore the Missouri River and to establish a link between it and the Pacific Ocean. In addition, he plotted the course of the Corps of Discovery and provided data on peripheral [adjoining] areas from the best native information he could obtain. Clark's efforts are a model of cartographic excellence, and his example was admired and emulated [copied] by generations of explorers and mapmakers. His legacy [contribution] is more than merely the maps he drew; it is the high standard of craftsmanship he set in executing [creating] them."

sick, probably from the unfamiliar food they had eaten, or perhaps because they had eaten too much after being hungry so long.

The next morning, Clark sent out hunters to get meat for those still struggling over the mountains. When they came back empty-handed, Clark bought food from the Indians and sent Reuben Field back with it. Then he and the others set out to find Twisted Hair, a Nez Percé chief who the Indians said knew the best route to the Columbia River. They arrived at his village after dark, and were received in a kindly manner.

If the Nez Percé had been hostile, Clark and his men, in their weakened condition, could easily have been killed.

There may have been such a plan, but Watkuweis, an elderly woman in Twisted Hair's village, advised against it. James P. Ronda relates the story:

> Watkuweis, whose name meant "returned from a far country," had been captured by Blackfeet or Atsina raiders sometime late in the eighteenth century. Taken into Canada, she had been purchased by a trader and had lived for several years among whites before finding her way home. Watkuweis had been treated well and had never lost her favorable impression of whites. When Clark came to Twisted Hair's camp, Watkuweis urged her people to treat the expedition with all hospitality.[63]

With the Nez Percé

The same day on which Clark pushed ahead to find food, Lewis and the main party dined on portable soup, bear oil, and candles made of tallow (animal fat). Over the next couple of days, they struggled slowly through the snow, eating anything they could locate. They found the horse meat Clark had left for them, and hungrily devoured it. On September 22, Reuben Field met them with fish and camas bread. Even though they were cautioned to eat sparingly, they were too hungry to heed the warning. Soon, they were all sick, too.

But they were out of the mountains at last. It had taken eleven days to make the crossing—eleven of the worst days in the entire trip. Not one of the diary writers mentions Sacagawea and the baby during the painful trip over the Bitterroot Mountains, but they, too, survived. Clark returned from his visit with Twisted Hair that same evening, and for a change, he had good news. It appeared to be possible to continue the journey by water. The nearby Clearwater River (which they called the Kooskooskee) would take them to the Snake and then to the Columbia.

First, however, canoes had to be made. For that job, they established Canoe Camp on the river, a few miles from Twisted Hair's village. Tasks that had once been fairly easy were now almost beyond them: "the party in general are So weak and feeble that we git along Slow with the canoes," Private Whitehouse wrote on September 30. Because their small axes were almost useless, they used the Indian method of hollowing the logs: "built fires on Several of the canoes to burn them out," Whitehouse continued, "found that they burned verry well."[64]

The Nez Percé agreed to look after the expedition's thirty-nine horses while the explorers were gone. In addition, Chief Twisted Hair and Tetoharsky, another Nez Percé chief, promised to guide them to the Columbia River. On October 7, almost two weeks after crossing the Rockies, the Corps of Discovery launched the newly completed dugout canoes into the Clearwater River.

The Clearwater was shallow, but swift and winding. On the second day out, one of the canoes hit a rock. All those aboard escaped unharmed, and the canoe was repaired. Shortly afterward, the Shoshone guide and his son left the expedition without a word to anyone. Perhaps Toby and the youth had been frightened by the canoe accident, or maybe they were just homesick. No one ever found out.

On October 10, the expedition reached the Snake River. On this rapids-

On October 10, 1805, the expedition arrived at the Snake River. This detailed sketch represents the confluence of the Snake and Columbia Rivers.

filled stream, several mishaps occurred, but no one was injured. A couple of days before reaching the confluence of the Snake and Columbia Rivers, the captains sent the two Nez Percé chiefs ahead to announce their arrival to the local tribes. Now they were in an area in which the Indian cultures were completely different from any they had encountered so far, and few, if any, of the Indians had ever seen white men. Many times during the next several months the Corps would be thankful for Sacagawea and her child, whose presence often calmed the uneasy Indians.

Twisted Hair and Tetoharsky fulfilled their advance mission well. When the expedition arrived at the confluence on October 16, the Indians put on a grand show. "After we had our camp fixed and fires made," Clark wrote, "a Chief came from this camp which was about ¼ of a mile up the Columbia river at the head of about 200 men singing and beeting on their drums . . . and keeping time to the musik they formed a half circle around us and Sung for Some time."[65] The captains smoked with their hosts and handed out presents and medals to the chiefs.

The Corps stayed at the confluence a few days, mending equipment and getting information about the route ahead. On October 18, they resumed their journey. Traveling on the Columbia River, they moved through barren plains where firewood was scarce and there was little game. Even so, they were in no danger of starving. Plenty of food was available from Indians who daily lined the banks to see the strange white men. The food was often unfamiliar to them, but it satisfied their hunger. Some of the expedition members even began eating fat dogs, which the Indians raised for food. Others (including Clark) resisted at first, but by the time they reached the ocean, practically everyone was eating the dog meat.

Wild Water on the Columbia

If the Corps members thought traveling with the current was going to be easy, they were soon disappointed. The flat plains through which the river had been flowing began to give way to a broken landscape. On October 22 they reached the first area of falls and rapids (today called Celilo Falls), which had to be portaged. Since this was a major fishing and trading location, Indians crowded the banks to watch the proceedings. Sergeant Gass described the portage in his diary:

> About 3 miles lower down we came to the first falls or great rapids; and had 1300 yards of portage over bad ground. All our baggage was got over this evening and we encamped with it. . . . At 9 o'clock in the forenoon [the next day] all hands, but three left to keep camp, went up and took the canoes over to the south side. . . . Here we had to drag them 450 yards round the first pitch which is 20 feet perpen-

dicular. We then put them into the water and let them down the rest of the way by cords. The whole height of the falls is 37 feet 8 inches, in a distance of 1200 yards.[66]

Not far ahead was another turbulent stretch of water, where the mighty Columbia raced through a narrow rocky channel. Clark called it the Short Narrows. Their most valuable baggage (guns, ammunition, journals, etc.) was carried around, but there was no way to portage the heavy canoes. Taking terrible risks, they sailed them through the rapids, to the amazement of the Indians watching from the banks.

A few miles below the Short Narrows was a twelve-mile stretch of rough water that Clark called the Long Narrows (known today as The Dalles, Oregon). After this stretch, the river grew calmer and easier to navigate. Here, too, the expedition had

Waterfalls and rapids complicated the navigation of the Columbia River and, often, made portaging necessary.

entered a different geographical zone where the climate became foggy and rainy. The change was brought about by the presence of a range of volcanic mountains (later named the Cascades) whose snow-covered peaks rose thousands of feet into the sky. When the warm, moist air from the Pacific Ocean hit the mountains, it rose, then cooled, and dropped most of its moisture on the western slopes.

The Indian tribes changed, too. This was the territory of Chinook-speaking peoples. The Chinooks had been dealing with traders from England and Canada for a long time and were not in awe of white men. Sensing trouble, Twisted Hair and

The Lolo Trail Revisited

One hundred years after the Lewis and Clark expedition, Olin D. Wheeler and a companion named Wright retraced the route as nearly as possible. In this excerpt from The Trail of Lewis and Clark, 1804–1904, *Wheeler describes the route across the Bitterroot Mountains (later known as the Lolo Trail).*

"A great trail like the Lolo is much like a great trunk line [main line] of railway. Here and there, at certain and favorable places, will be found lines of parallel trails, like parallel railway sidings, all merging at some point, into the main track or trail; branch trails also, like branch lines, will now and again be found. So it was and is here. There are many parallel trails, some of them now dim and overgrown through age and disuse, and there are evidently two or three points where the divide itself may be crossed. The conditions of travel are the same whichever route one takes, and all the trails terminate at the same point, the beautiful summit prairie or the glades of Glade Creek, down which the party [Corps of Discovery] proceeded two miles and camped. I have plotted [mapped] the trail over the pass as seems to me to meet best all the conditions of the narrative [the expedition's journals], both going and returning.

Mr. Wright and I camped at the forks of Glade Creek where Lewis and Clark first came out upon it—in a bed of delicious ripe wild strawberries. . . . We explored Glade Creek valley and found that the creek had numerous affluents [tributaries], and there were old trails on each side of the valley all converging at our camp. We startled a fawn, on our tramp, and watched a beautiful skunk prowling about the creek bank, its long black and white bushy tail floating like a banner over it."

While expedition members attempt to secure the canoes, Lewis and Clark consider options for navigating the raging rapids.

Tetoharsky left the expedition, but not before advising the captains of a possible attack by the Chinooks. A military alert was immediately declared and ammunition was distributed. The rumor may have been untrue, or the show of force may have changed the Chinooks' minds, but nothing happened.

About thirty-five miles beyond the narrows, the river again broke up into furious rapids, which later would be called the Upper and Lower Cascades. The Upper Cascades (which Clark called "the Great Shute") were unnavigable, so both baggage and canoes had to be portaged over the rocky riverbanks. At the Lower Cascades, they again portaged the valuables, but the canoes were daringly rowed right through the churning rapids. By skill, luck, or both, everyone emerged safely.

Continuing down the river, the Corps of Discovery came upon a village of Skilloot (a Chinook band) who controlled trade in that area. The settlement was an impressive one of wooden houses and fine

canoes, which the Corps members admired very much. The Skilloot treated their visitors very hospitably.

Back on the river, they stopped for lunch on a small island. To their surprise, they were soon joined by a large band of warriors from the Skilloot village they had just visited. During a hastily arranged council, the Skilloot became aggressive. Somebody stole Clark's tomahawk pipe and a coat belonging to one of the men. The Corps members refused to let the Indians leave until they had searched the Chinook canoes and recovered the stolen articles. The incident ended without bloodshed, but it led each side to distrust and dislike the other.

Onward to the Pacific

Moving westward with the current, they hurried on toward the ocean. The river ahead was so broad, Clark mistakenly wrote in his journal on November 7 that the ocean was in sight. Several more storm-filled days were to pass, however, before the ocean was actually reached. High winds and waves forced them to camp in an inlet for several days. Rain fell constantly, and their already ragged clothes rotted on their backs. On November 14, some of the men were able to row Captain Lewis and a small party out of the inlet and reach a sandy beach. From there Lewis and his group hiked overland to the ocean.

When Lewis returned to camp a few days later, Clark announced that he was going to hike overland to the ocean and that those who wished to accompany him should be ready early the next morning. Only ten men chose to make the trip, the rest being content to see the mighty Pacific from a distance. Clark and his party explored the coast a few miles and then returned to camp. Both captains had hoped to encounter an American or British sailing vessel, but none appeared.

Cold, wet, and battered by strong winds from the ocean, the Corps of Discovery looked about for a place to spend the winter. They were depressed by the never-ending fog and rain, and days went by without a decision. Then, on November 23, a group of visiting Clatsop invited them to spend the winter near their village on the opposite (south) side of the river, where weather conditions were better and elk were plentiful.

Although some wanted to go back to the narrows where the climate was dry, the

The elaborate hats crafted by the Clatsop out of cedar bark effectively repelled rain.

An invaluable commodity, salt was necessary to preserve and flavor food. This sketch illustrates how ocean water was boiled in large kettles until it evaporated, yielding salt.

majority voted to accept the invitation of the Clatsop. Getting across the wide and stormy river caused further delays. It was not until December 7, 1805, that they arrived at a location selected by Captain Lewis. There, near a little river (in present-day Oregon), the men set about building a log fort which they named Fort Clatsop, in honor of their Indian neighbors.

Wintering at Fort Clatsop

The winter at Fort Clatsop was much different from the winter at Fort Mandan. There were no subzero temperatures to endure, but in some ways the damp, cloudy weather was worse. When the hunters were fortunate enough to kill deer or elk, the meat often spoiled before they could eat it. On Christmas Day 1805, Clark wrote, "our Diner concisted of pore Elk, So much Spoiled that we eate it thro' mear necessity."[67]

There was nothing to do but endure the discomforts of winter camp and prepare for departure in the spring. New clothing and moccasins had to be sewn from elk and deer hides. A supply of dried meat for the return trip had to be prepared. They also needed salt to preserve the meat and to make their daily food taste better. Consequently, a few miles from Fort Clatsop, a salt camp was set up where ocean water was boiled in large kettles until it evaporated, leaving the salt behind.

Those at the main camp worked on building the fort, which was completed on December 30, 1805. At last they had a

*apparently pointed Consisting of 6 par and termonating in
one (in this form.)
Serrate, or like
of a Whipsaw, each
...ating in a Smale subulate spine, being from 25 to 27 in Numb
...ried Smoth, plane and of a deep green, their points
tending obliquely toward the extremity of the rib or
common footstalk. I do not know the fruit or flow-
er of either. the 1st resembles a plant Common to many parts of the United States Called the Mountain
Holly —.
Tuesday February 13th 1806.
The Clatsop left us this morning at 11. I do not*

While at Fort Clatsop, Lewis and Clark were able to compile detailed notes about the plants and wildlife they encountered during their long trek. This sketch and accompanying description of an evergreen shrub were found in one of Clark's notebooks.

place where they could stay dry. The fort was fifty feet square with a row of rooms on two sides facing each other. In between was an open space twenty feet wide. A tall picket fence enclosed both ends, making the fort secure against the possibility of an Indian attack (none ever occurred). A small house to store meat was also constructed.

There was plenty of activity to break the monotony and ease the waiting. Indians visited frequently, and hunters and salt camp workers came in and out. The captains took advantage of the time to do paperwork. Lewis compiled extensive notes about wildlife, plants, Indian customs, and languages. Clark worked on the maps he had been constructing along the way.

One day, a beached whale was sighted on the seacoast south of the fort. This was good news because it meant that a different food source might be available, and everyone was very tired of elk. Clark decided to find the whale. Sacagawea had not yet seen the ocean, and when she heard of Clark's plans, she insisted on going along.

"Charbono and his Indian woman were also of the party," Lewis wrote on January 6, 1806, after Clark left. "She [Sacagawea] observed that she had traveled a long way with us to see the great waters, and now that monstrous fish was also to be seen, she thought it very hard [unfair] she could not be permitted to see either."[68]

By the time the party reached the whale, the Clatsop had already stripped it, and only a skeleton remained. However, Clark was able to buy 300 pounds of blubber, which prompted him to write, "Small as this Stock is I prise it highly; and thank providence for directing the whale to us; and think him much more kind to us than he was to jonah, having Sent this monster to be *Swallowed by us* in Sted of *Swallowing of us* as jonah's did."[69]

The winter passed slowly at Fort Clatsop. To raise the spirits of the crew, the captains set a departure date—April 1, 1806. Impatience overcame them, however, and on March 23, they abandoned Fort Clatsop forever to start the long journey home.

7 Going Home

The mouth of the Columbia River was discovered in 1792 by Robert Gray, an American sea captain. After that time, vessels from various nations frequently sailed up the Columbia bringing trade goods to the Indians in exchange for furs. Lewis and Clark hoped for the arrival of such a ship while they were at Fort Clatsop. Jefferson had even suggested a possible return by sea in his letter of instructions to Lewis:

> On your arrival on that coast endeavor to learn if there be any port within your reach frequented by the sea-vessels of any nation, & to send two of your trusty people back by sea. . . . with a copy of your notes: and should you be of the opinion that the return of your party by the way they went will be eminently [exceedingly] dangerous, then ship the whole, & return by sea, by the way either of cape Horn [around South America], or the cape of good Hope [around Africa], as you shall be able.[70]

Even if they didn't return home by sea, a trading ship could provide them

In 1792 American sea captain Robert Gray discovered the mouth of the Columbia River. This important discovery allowed vessels from other nations to sail up the Columbia and trade with the Indians.

Considered healers by the Indians because of their medical knowledge, Lewis and Clark used this fame to trade medicines and treatment for desperately needed goods during the return journey.

with much-needed trade goods and provisions before starting overland. However, no vessel came that winter. An American ship, *Lydia*, did sail into the Columbia in April 1806 after Lewis and Clark had already gone. Some historians believe the *Lydia* was also there in November while the Corps was at Fort Clatsop, but the evidence is not conclusive. At any rate, the captains never saw a ship, and the Indians never spoke of one.

Up the Columbia

The eastward journey began with the spring thaw on March 23, 1806. The return trip up the Columbia River, against the current, was very difficult. Getting past the cascades, rapids, and falls required great strength and resourcefulness. At the Upper Cascades a large dugout got away from the party and was smashed to pieces on the rocks. Game was scarce, and the Indians had little food to spare as the annual salmon run had not yet started.

When the party finally reached the plains of the Columbia, Lewis and Clark decided it would be easier to travel overland. For that they needed horses, but they had little to offer for them. Furthermore, the local Indians were not sympathetic to their plight, often stealing from them and treating them disrespectfully.

The Indians drove hard bargains, too. They were very fond of blue beads, but the expedition's supply had long since run out. To obtain horses, the captains had to trade their clothing, cooking kettles, and any other provisions they could spare. Throughout the journey, both captains had used the medical knowledge they possessed and the store of medicines they brought with them to treat illnesses among the Indians. They now fell back on the reputations they had earned as healers and began to trade medicines and treatment in exchange for the goods they needed so badly. Feeling a bit guilty about his doctor role, Clark wrote, "in our present situation I think it is pardonable to continue this deception for they will not give us any provisions without compensation in merchendize, and our stock is now reduced to a mear handfull."[71] He further justified his ploy by stating that the Indians were never given anything that would harm them.

The situation improved greatly when the expedition reached the friendly Walla Walla near the Snake River. Sergeant Ordway described a celebration given by the Walla Walla to honor their guests:

> about 300 of the natives assembled to our Camp we played the fiddle and danced a while the head chief told our officers that they Should [would] be lonesom when we left them and they wished to hear one of our meddicine Songs and try to learn it and wished us to learn one of theirs and it would make them glad. So our men Sang 2 Songs which appeared to take great affect on them. they tryed to learn Singing with us with a low voice. . . . they wished our men to dance with them So we danced among them and they were much pleased.[72]

The captains acquired some very fine horses from Walla Walla chief Yellept and his people. When they were ready to leave, the chief and his men helped transport the expedition's baggage across the Columbia River. Traveling overland, with horses instead of canoes, the expedition arrived back in the region of the Nez Percé villages the first week in May 1806.

Back with the Nez Percé

When Lewis and Clark had visited the Nez Percé villages on their way to the Pacific, Broken Arm, one of the principal chiefs, had been absent. On their return, Broken Arm invited them to his village, where they were treated very generously. Not wishing to impose on the chief's hospitality, however, they soon established their own camp near the Clearwater River. There they settled down to wait for the snow to melt in the Bitterroot Mountains.

During their stay, a dispute arose between their old friend Twisted Hair and another chief. The argument was over who had cared for the expedition's horses while the easterners were away. The captains smoothed over the squabble, and Twisted Hair eventually brought back all but two of the horses. Those two, he said, were taken by Toby and his son, who had guided the expedition over the Lolo Trail and left without payment.

Two of the expedition members experienced serious health problems while waiting for the snow to melt. Baptiste, the little son of Charbonneau and Sacagawea (whom Clark called "Pomp") became very sick with a swelling about the throat and jaw. For two weeks, the captains tended him anxiously. Although none of the diaries mentions Sacagawea during this time, E. G. Chuinard writes, "No doubt Sacagawea was a busy mother during the days of Pomp's severe illness, and his recovery must be attributed to [his] mother's care and his endurance and natural resistance, as well as to the prescriptions of the captain-physicians."[73]

Another member of the Corps, William Bratton, suffered so badly from back pain that he could barely stand. It had begun at Fort Clatsop, and on the trip back he had either lain in a canoe or ridden a horse because he could not walk. Private Shields had heard that such ailments could be helped by sweat baths, so he constructed one. Bratton stayed in the sweat bath as long as he could stand it, after which he was plunged into a cold creek. This process was repeated several times, and within a few days, he was walking without pain for the first time in months.

When the Indians heard about Bratton's recovery, they brought one of their

Private Bratton Takes a Sweat Bath

Corps member William Bratton became ill at Fort Clatsop. Unable to walk without great pain, he lay in a canoe or rode horseback all the way to the Nez Percé villages. When John Shields suggested a sweat bath, Bratton was eager to try it. Captain Lewis describes the process in this excerpt from Original Journals of Lewis and Clark, *edited by Reuben Gold Thwaites.*

"William Bratton still continues very unwell; he eats heartily [and] digests his food well, and has recovered his flesh [weight] almost perfectly yet is so weak in the loins that he is scarcely able to walk, nor can he sit upwright but with the greatest pain. we have tried every remidy which our engenuity could devise, or with which our stock of medicines furnished us, without effect. John Shields observed that he had seen men in a similar situation restored by violent sweats. Bratton requested that he might be sweated in the manner proposed by Shields to which he consented. Shields sunk a circular hole of 3 feet diamiter four feet deep in the earth. he kindled a large fire in the hole and heated well, after which the first was taken out [and] a seat placed in the center of the hole for the patient with a board at the bottom for his feet to rest on; some hoops of willow poles were bent in an arch crossing each over the hole, and on these several blankets were thrown forming a secure and thick orning [awning] of about 3 feet high. the patient being striped naked was seated under this orning in the hole and the blankets well secured on every side. the patient was furnished with a vessel of water which he sprinkles on the bottom and sides of the hole and by that means creates as much steam or vapor as he could possibly bear, in this situation he was kept about 20 minutes after which he was taken out and suddonly plunged in cold water twise and then was immediately returned to the sweat hole where he was continued three quarters of an hour longer then taken out covered up in several blankets and suffered [allowed] to cool gradually. during the time of his being in the sweat hole, he drank copious draughts [large amounts] of a strong tea of horse mint. . . . this experiment was made yesterday; Bratton feels himself much better and is walking about today and says he is nearly free from pain."

respected chiefs who had been unable to walk for years. The sweat process was repeated several times over the next few weeks, and the chief eventually regained the use of his arms and legs.

Modern doctors have scientific explanations for these recoveries, but for Lewis and Clark, it was enough that Bratton was again well and able to travel. Moreover, rightly or wrongly, the chief's recovery added to their reputations as healers.

With everyone healthy again, the captains decided to start across the Bitterroot Mountains. Tired of waiting for their Nez Percé guides, they left without them on June 14. After three miserable days floundering through deep snow, they admitted defeat. Lewis gloomily wrote, "this is the first time Since we have been on this long tour that we have ever been compelled to retreat or make a retragrade [backward] march."[74]

Sending a few men ahead to find the guides, the rest of the party returned to their encampment at the foot of the mountains. On June 24, they started out again, this time with reliable Indian guides. Six days later, they were on the other side of the Bitterroot Mountains, soaking their weary bodies in the hot springs they had passed on the way out. The next day, they were back at Traveller's Rest.

The Corps Separates

During the winter at Fort Clatsop, Lewis and Clark had worked out a plan to do some additional exploring. Lewis and a small group of men planned to travel northeast to the Great Falls of the Missouri. Leaving a few men at Great Falls to portage the baggage around the falls, Lewis and three men would explore Maria's River and try to make peace with the Blackfeet.

At the same time, Clark intended to go back down the Bitterroot Valley, cross the continental divide, and make his way back to the three forks of the Missouri. From there he would send several men down the Missouri to help Lewis's party portage around the falls. Clark and the rest of the party would follow the Yellowstone River to its junction with the Missouri. Everyone was to meet at, or near, the mouth of the Yellowstone in a few weeks.

Lewis's Trip

On July 3, Lewis wrote, "I took leave of my worthy friend and companion Capt. Clark and the party that accompanyed him. I could not avoid feeling much concern on this occasion although I hoped this seperation was only momentary."[75] Following trails the Indians had told them about (the guides had returned to their tribe), Lewis and seven men arrived without incident at the Great Falls about a week later. Leaving three men to portage the canoes and the cached goods around the falls, Lewis, Drouillard, and the Field brothers (Reuben and Joseph) went off to explore Maria's River. Lewis also intended to talk with the much-feared Blackfeet if he got the chance, even though he knew it was risky. Just how risky, he was soon to find out.

On July 26 Lewis's party suddenly came upon a group of eight Piegan Indians, a division of the Blackfoot tribe. (Lewis mistook them for Atsinas, who were allies of

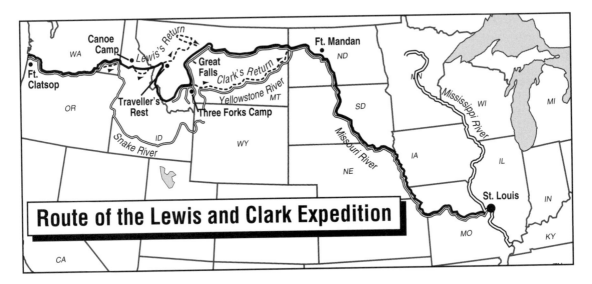

Route of the Lewis and Clark Expedition

the Blackfeet.) The initial meeting was very tense, but Lewis managed to convince the Indians of his peaceful mission. Through Drouillard's sign language, Lewis explained the intent of the United States to establish trade with the western tribes. Although Lewis did not realize it at the time, this was not good news for the Blackfeet. Because they could obtain guns from British traders, they controlled all the neighboring tribes who had no such source. If their enemies were able to obtain arms from the United States, the easy domination of the Blackfeet would end.

The following morning as the camp was waking up, the Indians suddenly grabbed the guns of Lewis's party. In the scuffle that followed, Lewis and his men managed to get their guns back, but Joseph Field stabbed one of the Indians to death. Their plot to seize the white man's guns having failed, the Indians tried to drive their horses off. Lewis gave chase and killed one of the Indians with his rifle when the man turned as if about to shoot. Before he died, the Indian did shoot at Lewis, but the shot passed over his head.

Lewis and his party quickly rounded up all the horses they could catch and left the scene. Fearing there might be a larger war party nearby, they returned as quickly as possible to the Missouri River. Arriving the next day after a hard ride, they were overjoyed to find the men they had left at the falls, as well as the men Clark had sent from the Three Forks coming along the river in five small canoes.

Both the pirogues that had been hidden months before were located, but the red pirogue was not fit for use. The white one was still serviceable, though, so with it and the canoes brought from the Three Forks, the men rowed swiftly down the Missouri toward their rendezvous with Clark. When they arrived at the mouth of the Yellowstone River, they found a note from Clark. He and his party had moved down the Missouri a few miles to find more game and escape the mosquitoes.

Lewis and his party hastened to find Clark, pausing only to hunt when a herd of elk was spotted onshore. It would have been better if they had passed up the elk. While hunting, Lewis was accidentally shot in the buttocks by Pierre Cruzatte, who had only one good eye. Sergeant Ordway recorded the incident as follows:

Peter [Pierre] Cruzatte a frenchman went out with Capt Lewis they Soon found a gangue of Elk in a thicket. Capt Lewis killed one and cruzatte killed two, and as he still kept fireing one of his balls hit Capt Lewis in his back side and the ball passed through one Side of his buttock and the ball went out of the other Side of the other buttock and lodged at his overalls

The Piegan Indians, a division of the Blackfoot tribe, obtained arms from British traders, which allowed them to easily dominate neighboring tribes. When news came that the United States wished to establish trade with western tribes, the Piegan feared that they would lose their advantage.

which wounded him bad. he instantly called to peter but Peter not answering he Supposd it to be Indians and run to the canoes and ordered the men to their armes. they were in readiness in a moment and Capt Lewis attempd to go back for battle but being faint the men purswaded him not to go himself but the party run out found Cruzatte and he had Seen no Indians then peter knew that it must have been him [who shot Lewis] tho an exidant [accident].[76]

Lewis believed Cruzatte knew from the first what he had done, but was so horrified that he wouldn't answer when Lewis called out to him. Although Lewis's wound was not life-threatening it was very painful and made traveling very difficult.

Clark's Trip

On the same day that Lewis left Traveller's Rest, Clark and his party moved south through the Bitterroot Valley. To save time, they crossed the continental divide several miles north of the Lemhi Pass, where they had crossed on the way out. Back at their cache on the Jefferson River, they dug up the things they had buried months before and found many items still intact.

All but one of the dugouts they had hidden were still usable. Heading back to the three forks of the Missouri, some of the men traveled in the canoes, while others took the horses overland. Both groups arrived on July 13. Later that day, nine men continued down the Missouri in the canoes commanded by Sergeant Ordway. Their mission was to meet Lewis's men at the Great Falls and help portage the canoes and baggage around that obstacle.

Sergeant Patrick Gass and His Diary

During the expedition Sergeant Gass kept a diary, which was published in 1807. Before publication, the wording was changed considerably because it showed the author's almost total lack of formal education. The original diary has been lost, so historians regard the edited version with caution. These observations about Gass and his diary, A Journal of the Voyages and Travels of a Corps of Discovery, *are taken from the introduction by Earle R. Forrest.*

"Gass and Sgt. Ordway were in Capt. Russell Bissell's company of the First Infantry, stationed at Fort Kaskaskia in the fall of 1803 when Capt. Meriwether Lewis came in search of volunteers for an expedition to the Pacific Coast. Gass is described at this period of his life as about five feet seven, broad-chested and strong. Such a journey, through a country much of which had never been seen by a white man, appealed to his adventurous spirit, and he was one of the first to volunteer along with Ordway. Capt. Bissell released the latter, but he refused consent for Gass to join. Gass was a good soldier and a first rate carpenter—scarce combinations on the frontier—and his Captain felt that he could ill-afford the loss of so valuable a man. Gass's determination was supreme, however, and after a private interview with Capt. Lewis, the leader used his authority to override Bissell, and Sergeant Gass became the carpenter of the Lewis and Clark Expedition.

Gass kept a diary during the entire Expedition, and he expected to realize something from its sale for publication when he returned. As his education was limited to fourteen days in school, and he had practically learned to read and write through his own application, the diary was in rather crude form. . . .

The diary he had planned to sell at some profit was published in 1807, and while it met with enthusiastic acceptance by the public, Gass received only 100 copies as his share of the venture. The manuscript was edited by David McKeehan, a school teacher of Wellsburg [Virginia], and was published by Zadok Kramer at Pittsburgh."

[Gass outlived all the other expedition members, dying in 1870 at the age of 98 years and 8 months.]

The next day, Clark and the rest of the party moved overland with the horses to find the Yellowstone River. They traveled once more through territory that Saca-gawea remembered from her childhood, and the Shoshone woman was able to assist Clark in finding the way. Shortly after reaching the Yellowstone, Clark's party made dugout canoes to travel on the river. According to a plan made at Traveller's Rest, the horses were to be driven to the Mandan villages by Sergeant Pryor and a small group of men. At the Mandans, the horses would be exchanged for trade goods. These goods would then be given to the Sioux chiefs on the return trip to persuade some of them to visit the president in Washington.

Unfortunately, half the horse herd was stolen before Pryor even got started, and the other half was stolen a few days later while he and his men were on the way to the Mandan villages with them! "Horses were symbolic of wealth among all the Upper Missouri tribes in Lewis and Clark's time," writes historian John C. Ewers. "Poor but ambitious young men found that the simplest way to acquire horses was to steal them from alien peoples—whether Indians or whites. There was no stigma

[shame] attached to this action. Rather the theft of a horse was recognized as a minor war honor."[77]

Clark's trip down the Yellowstone River took him and his party through a land of great beauty, teeming with wildlife. A particularly notable natural feature was an isolated rock tower along the river (a few miles east of Billings, Montana, today). Clark named it Pompy's Tower for Sacagawea's son. Hiking to the tower, he climbed partway up and carved his name into the rock. The inscription may still be seen there, protected by a heavy glass cover.

For the most part, the Yellowstone exploration was a peaceful trip with few problems (except the theft of the horses). Clark regretted that he was not able to make contact with the Crow Indians who lived in that area, but they kept their distance, perhaps because they had stolen the horses. On August 3, 1806, the party

Traveling through familiar territory, Sacagawea guides the Lewis and Clark expedition during their journey home.

of nine people entered the Missouri River to find that no one else had arrived.

After losing the horses, Pryor and his group had made bull boats out of bent willow sticks and covered them with buffalo hide. In those swift but hard-to-manage boats, they had caught up with a surprised and disappointed Captain Clark on August 8. Without horses to exchange for gifts, the plan for pacifying the Sioux was doomed to failure. But at least Pryor and the men were all right.

A few days later there was much more to rejoice about. Sergeant Gass, who was with Lewis's party, wrote on August 12, "We proceeded on and at 10 o'clock overtook Captain Clarke and his party, all in good health. . . . and now, (thanks to God) we are all together again in good health, except Capt. Lewis, and his wound is not dangerous."[78]

The Reunited Corps Returns Home

A few days later, the reunited Corps of Discovery arrived at the Mandan villages, where they received a rousing welcome. When they left on August 17, they were accompanied by Chief Sheheke and his family, whom Clark had persuaded to travel to Washington to meet the president. No other chiefs would go because of their fear of the Sioux. The captains were discouraged that all their peacemaking efforts among the tribes had come to nothing.

The Charbonneau family remained at the Mandan villages where Lewis and Clark had met them so many months before. Clark invited them to visit St. Louis, offering to educate little Pomp there as

soon as he was old enough to leave his parents. They also left behind expedition member John Colter, who received permission to join a fur trapping party.

Except for another shouting match with the Teton Sioux, the rest of the trip was uneventful. Lewis's condition improved daily. Near Council Bluffs, the men stopped at Sergeant Floyd's grave to pay their respects. Finding that the grave had been opened, they refilled it and moved on. As they got closer to St. Louis, several traders coming up the river supplied them with food and badly needed clothing.

When the men reached the first little settlement outside St. Louis, everyone was astonished that they were still alive. They had been given up for lost long ago. At St. Charles, where they stayed overnight, they were warmly received by the townspeople. On Tuesday, September 23, 1806, Sergeant Ordway wrote:

we Set out after breakfast and procd on Soon arrived at the Mouth of the Missourie entered the Mississippi River and landed at River deboise where we wintered in 1804. . . . we delayed a Short time and about 12oClock we arived in Site of St Louis fired three Rounds as we approached the Town and landed oppocit the center of the Town, the people gathred on the Shore and Hizzared three cheers. we unloaded the canoes and carried the baggage all up to a store house in Town [and] drew out the canoes then the party all considerable much rejoiced that we have the Expedition Completed and now look for boarding in Town and wait for our Settlement [the pay and land grants promised them] and then we entend to return to

Dear Mr. Jefferson: We're Back!

One of the first things Captain Lewis did after returning to St. Louis was write a long letter to President Jefferson. The outgoing mail was held up several hours to allow Lewis to finish, but even so the letter took nearly a month to get to Washington. These excerpts from Lewis's letter are taken from Letters of the Lewis and Clark Expedition, *edited by Donald Jackson.*

"Sir,   St. Louis September 23rd 1806

It is with pleasure that I announce to you the safe arrival of myself and party at 12 OClk. today at this place with our papers and baggage. In obedience to your orders, we have penitrated the Continent of North America to the Pacific Ocean. . . . [Lewis continues for several pages telling Jefferson about their discoveries. He then moves on to personal matters.] I have prevailed on the great Cheif of the Mandan nation to accompany me to Washington; he is now with my frind and colligue Capt. Clark at this place, in good health and sperits, and very anxious to proceede.

With rispect to the exertions and services rendered by that esteemable man Capt. William Clark in the course of late voyage I cannot say too much; if sir any credit be due for the success of that arduous [difficult] enterprize in which we have been mutually engaged, he is equally with myself entitled to your consideration and that of our common country. [He then tells Jefferson the route he is taking back to Washington.] . . . I am very anxious to learn the state of my friends in Albemarle [the county in Virginia where Lewis lived] particularly whether my mother is yet living. I am with every sentiment of esteem Your Obt. and very Humble servent.

Meriwether Lewis Capt.
1st. U.S. Regt. Infty."

our native homes to See our parents once more as we have been so long from them.—finis [end].[79]

The next day, Captain Lewis wrote a letter to President Jefferson, informing him that the members of the Corps of Discovery had accomplished their mission: they had followed the Missouri River to its source; they had reached the Pacific Ocean and returned.

8 Outcomes

The departure of the Corps of Discovery from St. Louis in the spring of 1804 had caused very little excitement. When the men returned to St. Louis, two years and thousands of miles later, they quickly became celebrities. At St. Louis and later in Washington, they were honored at ceremonies, parties, and balls.

Return to Civilian Life

Eventually, even heroes must go back to the business of everyday living. "It can easily be imagined that for many of the men the return to civilian life was a difficult time of adjustment," Charles G. Clarke writes. "Then as today, men have had a problem adjusting to sudden fame and adulation [praise], and not everyone can successfully take it in stride. We can understand then, if a few of these men fell by the wayside."[80]

Captain Meriwether Lewis

Unfortunately, Captain Lewis was one of those who "fell by the wayside." At first everything went well. Back in Washington, he was honored at ceremonies and entertained at parties and balls. In Philadelphia he visited the professors who had in-

structed him prior to the expedition. While there, he started making arrangements to have the journals published.

As the excitement faded, Lewis began experiencing personal problems. Now thirty-three years old, he hoped to marry,

Upon the expedition's return, Meriwether Lewis was revered as a national hero. Unfortunately, his fame and subsequent governorship were not enough to overcome his personal problems and bouts of depression.

News of the Corps' Safe Return

The news that the Corps of Discovery had returned safely was printed and reprinted in the nation's newspapers. This excerpt from Original Journals of the Lewis and Clark Expedition, *edited by Reuben Gold Thwaites, gives a sample of an early newspaper report of the expedition's return.*

"The first newspaper notices of the return of the expedition appear to have been based on letters from residents of St. Louis, or others who were personally interested in the affair. . . . Extract from letter to editors of the Baltimore Federal Gazette, under date of St. Louis, September 23, 1806:

'Concerning the safe arrival of Messrs. Lewis and Clark, who went 2 years and 4 months ago to explore the Missouri, to be anxiously wished for by everyone, I have the pleasure to mention that they arrived here about one hour ago, in good health, with only the loss of one man who died. They visited the Pacific Ocean, which they left on the 27th [23rd] of March last. They would have been here about the 1st of August, but for the detention they met with from snow and frost in crossing mountains on which are eternal snows. Their journal will no doubt be not only importantly interesting to us all, but a fortune for the worthy and laudable adventurers. When they arrived 3 cheers were fired. They really have the appearance of Robinson Crusoes—dressed entirely in buckskins. We shall know all very soon—I have had no particulars yet.'"

but none of the women he courted consented to become his wife. In 1807 he was appointed governor of the Upper Louisiana Territory, but he did not report to his office in St. Louis for almost a year afterward. When he finally took over the governor's job, he entered a world of politics for which he was not well fitted.

A few months later, entangled in office problems, he decided to go to Washington and get things straightened out. He was also concerned about the journals. Almost three years had passed since the return of the expedition, and he had done nothing more to prepare them for publication. Leaving St. Louis in a troubled frame of mind, he never reached Washington.

On October 11, 1809, Meriwether Lewis died of gunshot wounds at Grinder's Stand [wayside inn] in Tennessee. Whether he shot himself or was murdered in a robbery has been a matter of controversy ever since. Knowing that their friend occasionally suffered from periods of depression, both Thomas Jefferson and William Clark were convinced that Lewis had died by his own hand. Others disagree, saying the circumstances of his death were very suspicious, and that highway robberies were not uncommon on the Natchez Trace [trail] on which he was traveling.

Captain William Clark

Captain Clark's uppermost thought when he returned to St. Louis was of Julia Hancock, a young lady who lived in Virginia. As soon as possible after returning, he went back to propose to her. She consented, but due to new responsibilities Clark had taken after the expedition, they were not married until January 5, 1808. As a reward for his service in the Corps of Discovery, Clark was appointed brigadier general of militia for the Upper Louisiana Territory and superintendent of Indian affairs at St. Louis. Returning to St. Louis, he took up his new duties with enthusiasm. Historian David Lavender writes:

Clark's concluding years were the antithesis [opposite] of Lewis's. In 1813 he was named territorial governor and held that office until the state of Missouri was created in 1820. Though defeated in the first election for state governor, he continued as superintendent of Indian affairs. Whether dealing with whites or Indians or both together, he sought to settle controversies by conciliation [peaceful means]. He was imposingly proportioned [large in body],

William Clark (right) proposed to Julia Hancock (left) upon his return from the expedition, but the couple postponed their marriage until January 5, 1808.

dignified, trustworthy, and respected. Most Indians liked him, called him Red Head Chief and, whenever circumstances brought them to St. Louis, eagerly visited him and the Indian Hall he had erected on his estate.[81]

William Clark and Julia had four sons and a daughter. After Julia died, Clark married Harriet Kennerly, a widow, and they had two sons. Clark died in 1838 at the age of sixty-eight.

The Charbonneau Family

Sacagawea and Charbonneau brought their son, Baptiste, to St. Louis around 1810. They returned to the Dakotas in 1811, leaving the six-year-old Baptiste in William Clark's care. They traveled aboard a boat that was also carrying Henry M. Brackenridge, an explorer and writer. Brackenridge wrote:

> We had on board a Frenchman named Charbonet, with his wife, an Indian woman of the Snake [Shoshone] nation, both of whom had accompanied Lewis and Clark to the Pacific, and were of great service. The woman, a good creature, of a mild and gentle disposition, greatly attached to the whites, whose manners and dress she tries to imitate, but she had become sickly, and longed to revisit her native country; her husband, also, who had spent many years amongst the Indians, was become weary of a civilized life.[82]

Sacagawea died in 1812 at Fort Manuel in present-day South Dakota. John Luttig, clerk at Fort Manuel, made a notation in his journal on December 20, 1812, saying, "this Evening the Wife of Charbonneau a Snake [Shoshone] Squaw, died of a putrid fever [probably typhoid fever] she was a good and the best Women in the fort, age abt 25 years she left a fine infant girl."[83] In 1955 a notebook kept by Clark during the years 1825–1828 was found. On the cover he had written, "Se car ja we au Dead."[84]

When Fort Manuel was closed after an Indian attack, Luttig brought the infant girl, named Lisette, to St. Louis. Court records show that she was adopted by Captain Clark, but nothing is known of her later life.

In spite of these documents, many writers and novelists have insisted that Sacagawea did not die in 1812. They say she wandered throughout the West for a time, eventually settling on a reservation in Wyoming. There she supposedly lived to be one hundred years old. The evidence for these claims is based largely on word-of-mouth stories handed down over the years, and on interviews with an elderly Indian woman who claimed to be Sacagawea.

The later lives of Sacagawea's husband and son can be traced clearly. After the expedition, Charbonneau continued to work as an interpreter. His name appears in the records of many explorers and fur traders. In 1839, at the age of eighty, he came to St. Louis to collect money the government owed him. He died in the early 1840s, and his estate was settled by his son Jean Baptiste in 1843.

Jean Baptiste was educated in St. Louis and later adopted by William Clark. As a young man, he traveled throughout Europe with a young German prince who had come to America on an exploring trip. On his return to America, he accompanied many famous explorers and fur traders as a guide and interpreter. He died in Oregon in 1866 at the age of sixty-one.

The Later Life of Baptiste Charbonneau

Jean Baptiste Charbonneau, the son of Sacagawea and Toussaint Charbonneau, had a most unusual life. He spent his first few months on the trail with the Lewis and Clark expedition. As a young boy, he was adopted by Captain Clark and educated in St. Louis. Historian Harold P. Howard describes what happened to Baptiste afterward in this excerpt from Sacajawea.

"In 1823, Prince Paul of Wurttemberg, a twenty-year-old explorer, was given permission to travel up the Missouri River. He met both Baptiste and old Charbonneau. In the prince's account of his travels, which was published in 1835, he described his first meeting with Baptiste, near the mouth of the Kaw River [in Kansas], on June 21, 1823:

'Here I found a youth of sixteen [Baptiste was actually eighteen at the time], whose mother was of the tribe of Sho-sho-ne, or Snake Indians, and who had accompanied the Messrs. Lewis and Clark to the Pacific ocean in the years 1804 to 1806 as interpretress. This Indian woman was married to the French interpreter of the expedition, Toussaint Charbonneau by name. Charbonneau rendered me service also, some time later in the same capacity, and Baptiste, his son (the youth of sixteen) of whom I made mention above, joined me on my return and followed me to Europe, and has remained with me ever since.'

When he returned from Europe, Baptiste was well educated and could converse fluently in German, Spanish, French, and English. Despite his Continental education, on his return to America he apparently resumed life on the frontier. Up to 1846 western narratives mention him frequently and identify him clearly."

Looking Backward: An Evaluation of the Lewis and Clark Expedition

The significance of a historic event cannot be fairly evaluated until many years after its occurrence. Historian Henry Adams, writing in 1889, attached little importance to the Lewis and Clark expedition. "Creditable as these expeditions were to American energy and enterprise," he wrote, "they added little to the stock of science or wealth. . . . The crossing of the continent was a great feat but was nothing more."[85] A century later, many historians disagree, feeling that the expedition influenced future events in American history in several ways.

Although it would be several decades before wagon trains started pushing overland, the Lewis and Clark expedition took some of the fear and mystery out of the uncharted West. The journey undertaken by the Corps had been long and hard, but it had succeeded. The party had even included a woman and a baby! For the most part, the encounters with Indian tribes had been friendly, a matter of great concern to white people on the frontier. Moreover, the natural wonders described by Corps members stirred the blood of many restless men and women who longed to see those marvels for themselves.

In addition, the expedition ushered in the American fur trade that took place during the next few decades by bringing back good news about the abundance of beaver, and about waterways on which to transport the fur, and the fur trade had a side effect that was probably more impor-tant than the trade itself. While trapping beaver, many hardy "mountain men" roamed all over the West. In doing so, they greatly expanded the geographical data acquired by Lewis and Clark. Trappers often brought new information to William Clark, who continued to work on mapping the region west of the Mississippi long after the expedition.

The Expedition Strengthened America's Claim to the Oregon Country

In the early nineteenth century, both Great Britain and the United States competed for possession of the Oregon Territory, particularly the Columbia River region. The British felt it was rightfully theirs because they had been there a long time and had established many fur trading posts. The United States had a foothold in

Decades after Lewis and Clark's landmark expedition, pioneers migrate west. The expedition not only increased curiosity in this new frontier, it dispelled many of the fears surrounding the long journey.

the area, however, because Robert Gray, who sailed to the mouth of the Columbia River in 1792, was an American.

This claim was greatly strengthened when Lewis and Clark traveled through the Oregon Territory and down the Columbia River to the Pacific. It was further strengthened when John Jacob Astor established a fur trading post on the Oregon coast in 1811, only five years after the expedition. "It was the journey of Lewis and Clark that gave the American people a conviction that Oregon was theirs," Bernard DeVoto says, "and this conviction was more important than the claim. And . . . the establishment of Fort Astoria by Astor's party won the British-American race to the Pacific."[86]

The Expedition Affected the Future of the Indians

The Corps of Discovery owed a heavy debt to many of the Indian tribes they encountered along the way. Without the periodic assistance of Indians they might not have survived. Food, shelter, information, horses, guides, and many unnamed kindnesses were provided by Indians at one time or another. In turn Lewis and Clark treated the Indians with respect and tried to learn as much as possible about their cultures, as Jefferson had requested. With a few exceptions, relationships with Indian groups were friendly and positive.

Nevertheless, when Lewis and Clark "opened" the West, they sowed the seeds of destruction for the Indian nations residing there. Lewis and Clark's mission was not undertaken primarily for the benefit of the continent's earliest inhabitants. Its immediate purposes were to open the Missouri River for American traders and

to discourage the Indians from trading with the British. Its long-range purpose was to evaluate the prospects for future white settlement.

When the expedition neared St. Louis, the group stopped at Fort Bellfontaine to let Chief Sheheke and his family obtain new clothing. James P. Ronda writes:

As the Indian [Chief Sheheke] searched through the stacks of calico shirts, fancy handkerchiefs, and colored beads, he symbolized the first fruits of the Lewis and Clark expedition. The explorers brought Indian America face to face with the Industrial Revolution and a rising American empire. . . . The Mandan chief, dressed in the best the young Republic could afford, did not know how much those explorers had forever changed his world.[87]

In 1806 the new American nation, often scorned by Europeans, needed a dose of national pride. Lewis and Clark and the Corps of Discovery provided it. On December 2, 1806, President Jefferson sent the following message to Congress:

The expedition of Messrs. [Messieurs: French plural form of "Mister"] Lewis and Clarke, for exploring the river Missouri, and the best communication from that to the Pacific Ocean, has had all the success which could have been expected. They have traced the Missouri nearly to its source, descended the Columbia to the Pacific Ocean, ascertained with accuracy the geography of that interesting communication across our continent, learned the character of the country, of its commerce, and inhabitants; and it is

The success of the Lewis and Clark expedition depended largely on the generosity of the many Indian tribes who offered guidance, shelter, and supplies to the explorers.

but justice to say that Messrs Lewis and Clarke, and their brave companions, have by this arduous service deserved well of their country.[88]

If Lewis and Clark had not crossed the continent, someone else would have. It was not the journey alone that made the expedition an enduring part of American history, but the people themselves and the relationships that developed among them.

It would be hard to imagine a more colorful group—two young captains with very different personalities, a mixed crew from diverse cultural backgrounds, a Negro slave, a French/Indian interpreter, a young Indian girl carrying a baby on her back, and a big black dog!

As interesting as the individuals were, it was the harmonious relationships among them that often made the difference between success and failure. In good times, they danced and sang together. In bad times they drew close to one another and endured what had to be endured. The friendship between the captains, the loyalty and dedication of the men, the encouragement of Sacagawea, the fiddle playing of Cruzatte, the excited barking of a dog, the surprising sound of a child's voice—all these things worked together to make the Lewis and Clark expedition a one-of-a-kind event in American history.

Notes

Chapter 1: The Lewis and Clark Expedition: Its Roots and Purposes

1.   Bernard DeVoto, ed., *The Journals of Lewis and Clark*. Boston: Houghton Mifflin, 1953.

2.   Quoted in Donald Jackson, ed., *Letters of the Lewis and Clark Expedition*. Urbana: University of Illinois Press, 1978.

3.   David Lavender, *The Way to the Western Sea: Lewis and Clark Across the Continent*. New York: Harper & Row, 1988.

4.   Quoted in Lavender, *The Way to the Western Sea*.

5.   Quoted in Merrill D. Peterson, ed., *Thomas Jefferson: Writings*. New York: The Library of America, 1984.

6.   Quoted in Peterson, ed., *Thomas Jefferson: Writings*.

7.   Quoted in Henry Adams, *History of the United States of America During the Administrations of Thomas Jefferson*. 1889. Reprint, New York: The Library of America, 1986.

Chapter 2: The Corps of Discovery: Getting Ready to Go

8.   E. G. Chuinard, *Only One Man Died: The Medical Aspects of the Lewis and Clark Expedition*. Glendale, CA: Arthur H. Clark, 1980.

9.   Quoted in Lavender, *The Way to the Western Sea*.

10.   John Bakeless, *Lewis and Clark: Partners in Discovery*. 1947. Reprint, New York: William Morrow, 1966.

11.   Charles G. Clarke, *The Men of the Lewis and Clark Expedition*. Glendale, CA: Arthur H. Clark, 1970.

12.   Clarke, *The Men of the Lewis and Clark Expedition*.

13.   Quoted in Milo M. Quaife, ed., *The Journals of Captain Meriwether Lewis and Sergeant John Ordway*. Madison, WI: State Historical Society, 1916.

14.   Quoted in Ernest Staples Osgood, *The Field Notes of Captain William Clark, 1803–1805*. New Haven, CT: Yale University Press, 1964.

15.   Quoted in Jackson, ed., *Letters of the Lewis and Clark Expedition*.

16.   Lavender, *The Way to the Western Sea*.

17.   Quoted in Jackson, ed., *Letters of the Lewis and Clark Expedition*.

18.   Quoted in Gary E. Moulton, ed., *The Journals of the Lewis and Clark Expedition*, vol. 2. Lincoln: University of Nebraska, 1983.

Chapter 3: The Journey: From Camp Wood to the Mandan Villages

19.   Lavender, *The Way to the Western Sea*.

20.   Quoted in Moulton, ed., *The Journals of the Lewis and Clark Expedition*, vol. 2.

21.   Quoted in Reuben Gold Thwaites, ed., *Original Journals of the Lewis and Clark Expedition, 1804–1806*, vol. 7. 1904-1905. Reprint, New York: Antiquarian Press, 1959.

22.   Quoted in Moulton, ed., *The Journals of the Lewis and Clark Expedition*, vol. 2.

23.   James P. Ronda, *Lewis and Clark Among the Indians*. Lincoln: University of Nebraska Press, 1984.

24.   Quoted in Moulton, ed., *The Journals of the Lewis and Clark Expedition*, vol. 2.

25.   Quoted in Quaife, ed., *The Journals of Captain Meriwether Lewis and Sergeant John Ordway*.

26.   DeVoto, ed., *The Journals of Lewis and Clark*.

27.   Quoted in DeVoto, ed., *The Journals of Lewis and Clark*.

28.   Ronda, *Lewis and Clark Among the Indians*.

29. Bakeless, *Lewis and Clark: Partners in Discovery*.

Chapter 4: From the Mandan Villages to the Great Falls of the Missouri

30. Quoted in Moulton, ed., *The Journals of the Lewis and Clark Expedition*, vol. 3.

31. Quoted in Moulton, ed., *The Journals of the Lewis and Clark Expedition*, vol. 3.

32. Quoted in Moulton, ed., *The Journals of the Lewis and Clark Expedition*, vol. 4.

33. Quoted in Moulton, ed., *The Journals of the Lewis and Clark Expedition*, vol. 4.

34. Quoted in DeVoto, ed., *The Journals of Lewis and Clark*.

35. Quoted in DeVoto, ed., *The Journals of Lewis and Clark*.

36. Quoted in Thwaites, ed., *Original Journals of the Lewis and Clark Expedition*, vol. 2.

37. Quoted in Thwaites, ed., *Original Journals of the Lewis and Clark Expedition*, vol. 2.

38. Quoted in DeVoto, ed., *The Journals of Lewis and Clark*.

39. Quoted in Quaife, ed., *The Journals of Captain Meriwether Lewis and Sergeant John Ordway*.

40. Quoted in Quaife, ed., *The Journals of Captain Meriwether Lewis and Sergeant John Ordway*.

41. Quoted in DeVoto, ed., *The Journals of Lewis and Clark*.

42. Quoted in DeVoto, ed., *The Journals of Lewis and Clark*.

43. Lavender, *The Way to the Western Sea*.

44. David Freeman Hawke, *Those Tremendous Mountains: The Story of the Lewis and Clark Expedition*. New York: W. W. Norton, 1980.

Chapter 5: From the Great Falls of the Missouri to the Lolo Trail

45. Quoted in Thwaites, ed., *Original Journals of the Lewis and Clark Expedition*, vol. 2.

46. Quoted in Thwaites, ed., *Original Journals of the Lewis and Clark Expedition*, vol. 2.

47. Quoted in DeVoto, ed., *The Journals of Lewis and Clark*.

48. Quoted in DeVoto, ed., *The Journals of Lewis and Clark*.

49. Quoted in Thwaites, ed., *Original Journals of the Lewis and Clark Expedition*, vol. 7.

50. Quoted in Moulton, ed., *The Journals of the Lewis and Clark Expedition*, vol. 5.

51. Quoted in Moulton, ed., *The Journals of the Lewis and Clark Expedition*, vol. 5.

52. Quoted in Quaife, ed., *The Journals of Captain Meriwether Lewis and Sergeant John Ordway*.

53. Quoted in Moulton, ed., *The Journals of the Lewis and Clark Expedition*, vol. 5.

54. Quoted in Moulton, ed., *The Journals of the Lewis and Clark Expedition*, vol. 5.

55. Lavender, *The Way to the Western Sea*.

56. Patrick Gass, *A Journal of the Voyages and Travels of a Corps of Discovery*. 1807. Reprint, with an introduction by Earle R. Forrest. Minneapolis: Ross and Haines, 1958.

57. Quoted in Moulton, ed., *The Journals of the Lewis and Clark Expedition*, vol. 5.

58. Quoted in DeVoto, ed., *The Journals of Lewis and Clark*.

59. Quoted in DeVoto, ed., *The Journals of Lewis and Clark*.

Chapter 6: From the Lolo Trail to the Pacific Ocean

60. Quoted in Moulton, ed., *The Journals of the Lewis and Clark Expedition*, vol. 6.

61. Quoted in Thwaites, ed., *Original Journals of the Lewis and Clark Expedition*, vol. 7.

62. Quoted in Moulton, ed., *The Journals of the Lewis and Clark Expedition*, vol. 6.

63. Ronda, *Lewis and Clark Among the Indians*.

64. Quoted in Thwaites, ed., *Original Journals of the Lewis and Clark Expedition*, vol. 7.

65. Quoted in DeVoto, ed., *The Journals of Lewis and Clark*.

66. Gass, *A Journal of the Voyages and Travels of*

a Corps of Discovery.

67. Quoted in Moulton, ed., *The Journals of the Lewis and Clark Expedition*, vol. 6.

68. Quoted in Moulton, ed., *The Journals of the Lewis and Clark Expedition*, vol. 6.

69. Quoted in Moulton, ed., *The Journals of the Lewis and Clark Expedition*, vol. 6

Chapter 7: Going Home

70. Quoted in Jackson, ed., *Letters of the Lewis and Clark Expedition.*

71. Quoted in DeVoto, ed., *The Journals of Lewis and Clark.*

72. Quoted in Quaife, ed., *The Journals of Captain Meriwether Lewis and Sergeant John Ordway.*

73. Chuinard, *Only One Man Died.*

74. Quoted in Moulton, ed., *The Journals of the Lewis and Clark Expedition*, vol. 8.

75. Quoted in Moulton, ed., *The Journals of the Lewis and Clark Expedition*, vol. 8.

76. Quoted in Quaife, ed., *The Journals of Captain Meriwether Lewis and Sergeant John Ordway.*

77. John C. Ewers, *Indian Life on the Upper Missouri.* Norman: University of Oklahoma Press, 1968.

78. Gass, *A Journal of the Voyages and Travels of a Corps of Discovery.*

79. Quoted in Quaife, ed., *The Journals of Captain Meriwether Lewis and Sergeant John Ordway.*

Chapter 8: Outcomes

80. Clarke, *The Men of the Lewis and Clark Expedition.*

81. Lavender, *The Way to the Western Sea.*

82. Henry M. Brackenridge, *Views of Louisiana Together with a Journal of a Voyage Up the Missouri River, in 1811.* Pittsburgh: Cramer, Spear and Eichbaum, 1814.

83. John C. Luttig, *Journal of a Fur-Trading Expedition on the Upper Missouri 1812-1813.* St. Louis: Missouri Historical Society, 1920.

84. Quoted in Irving W. Anderson, "A Charbonneau Family Portrait," *The American West,* March/April 1980.

85. Henry Adams, *History of the United States of America During the Administrations of Thomas Jefferson.*

86. DeVoto, ed., *The Journals of Lewis and Clark.*

87. Ronda, *Lewis and Clark Among the Indians.*

88. Quoted in Thwaites, ed., *Original Journals of the Lewis and Clark Expedition*, vol. 5.

For Further Reading

Irving W. Anderson, "A Charbonneau Family Portrait," *The American West*, March/April 1980. Interesting article about the lives of Toussaint Charbonneau, Sacagawea, and their son, Baptiste. Many of the myths and untruths that have been written about the Charbonneau family are discussed. Colorfully illustrated.

Ralph K. Andrist, *To the Pacific with Lewis and Clark.* New York: American Heritage, 1967. Written for young adults, this volume is beautifully illustrated with paintings of historic scenes, photographs of places along the trail, and pictures of the original diaries, maps, and letters. Attractive and usable despite its age.

John Bakeless, *Lewis and Clark: Partners in Discovery.* 1947. Reprint, New York: William Morrow, 1966. This very readable narrative of the Lewis and Clark expedition includes interesting stories about President Jefferson and about the lives of the captains before and after the expedition.

Robert B. Betts, *In Search of York: The Slave Who Went to the Pacific with Lewis and Clark.* Boulder, CO: Associated University Press, 1985. One of the most interesting members of the Lewis and Clark expedition was York, the Negro slave who accompanied Clark on the expedition. The book presents what little is known about York's life before and after the expedition. Well illustrated with paintings and photographs.

Bernard DeVoto, ed., *The Journals of Lewis and Clark.* Boston: Houghton Mifflin, 1953. Excellent one-volume condensation of the original journals; retains the original wording and spelling. Provides an opportunity for advanced readers to discover what the journals actually said.

Julie Faneslow, *The Traveler's Guide to the Lewis and Clark Trail.* Helena, MT: Falcon Press, 1994. Popular new guidebook to the Lewis and Clark Trail which may be adapted to different vacation plans. Contains a suggested two-week trip over the trail if time is limited. Includes maps, photographs, and descriptions of interesting places to visit near the sites.

George Fronval and Daniel Dubois, *Indian Signs and Sign Language.* New York: Bonanza Books, 1985. Indian sign language played an important role on the Lewis and Clark expedition. This attractive book about sign language is illustrated with full-color photographs of American Indians in traditional costumes demonstrating hand signs.

Bil Gilbert, *The Trailblazers.* Alexandria, VA: Time-Life Books, 1973. One of the volumes in the Old West Series, this book about nineteenth-century American explorers includes a section on the Lewis and Clark expedition. Contains excellent illustrations.

David Freeman Hawke, *Those Tremendous Mountains: The Story of the Lewis and Clark Expedition.* New York: W. W. Norton, 1980. Advanced readers will enjoy this collection of exciting stories about the Lewis and Clark expedition. Includes tales about grizzly bears, Lewis's iron boat, the flash flood that almost drowned Captain Clark and the Charbonneau family, and many more.

Harold P. Howard, *Sacajawea*. Norman: University of Oklahoma Press, 1971. The author sorts through the myths about Sacagawea, her husband, and son, presenting only information that can be documented. The author's interesting writing style makes Sacagawea emerge as a real person.

David Muench, *Lewis and Clark Country*. Portland, OR: Beautiful America Publishing, 1978. Striking photographs of the Lewis and Clark Trail by a famous photographer fill the pages of this beautiful book. A short, but informative introduction precedes each section of photographs.

Francis Paul Prucha, *Indian Peace Medals in American History*. Madison, WI: State Historical Society, 1971. Like many other explorers and traders in the eighteenth and nineteenth centuries, Lewis and Clark presented medals made of silver or bronze to Indian leaders. Book contains photographs of medals of many types, including those distributed by Lewis and Clark.

Marshall Sprague, *So Vast So Beautiful a Land: Louisiana and the Purchase*. Boston: Little, Brown, 1974. Interesting account of the Louisiana Purchase with human-interest stories about the principal characters and their relationships to one another. Also includes a section on early exploration of the Louisiana Territory. For advanced readers.

We Proceeded On. The Official Publication of the Lewis and Clark Trail Heritage Foundation, P. O. Box 3434, Great Falls, MT 59403. This quarterly magazine carries many stimulating and unusual articles related to the Lewis and Clark expedition. It also offers book reviews, reports of the foundation's activities, and news of the latest discoveries related to the expedition. Well illustrated.

Additional Works Consulted

Henry Adams, *History of the United States of America During the Administrations of Thomas Jefferson*. 1889. Reprint, New York: The Library of America, 1986. A thorough study of U.S. history during the two presidential terms of Thomas Jefferson.

John Logan Allen, *Passage Through the Garden: Lewis and Clark and the Image of the American Northwest*. Urbana: University of Illinois Press, 1975. Contrasts many impressions held about the geography of the Northwest before the Lewis and Clark expedition with what the explorers actually found.

Irving W. Anderson, "A Charbonneau Family Portrait," *The American West*, March/April 1980. A well-documented article about the lives of Toussaint Charbonneau, Sacagawea, and their son, Baptiste. Sources of misinformation about the Charbonneau family are discussed in detail.

Roy E. Appleman, *Lewis and Clark: Historic Places Associated with Their Transcontinental Exploration (1804–06)*. St. Louis: Lewis and Clark Heritage Trail Foundation and the Jefferson National Expansion Historical Association, 1993. Recently reprinted, this popular National Park Service guide contains a brief history of the expedition and detailed descriptions of Lewis and Clark Trail sites. Liberally illustrated with photographs of the sites.

Henry M. Brackenridge, *Views of Louisiana Together with a Journal of a Voyage Up the Missouri River, in 1811*. Pittsburgh: Cramer, Spear and Eichbaum, 1814. In this journal, Brackenridge documents the presence of Sacagawea and Charbonneau on a riverboat traveling from St. Louis to Fort Manuel, in what is now South Dakota, in 1811.

E. G. Chuinard, *Only One Man Died: The Medical Aspects of the Lewis and Clark Expedition*. Glendale, CA: Arthur H. Clark, 1980. An interesting account by a physician of the illnesses, diseases, and accidents that occurred on the expedition and the treatments and remedies used for them. Also includes information about the practice of medicine in the early nineteenth century.

Charles G. Clarke, *The Men of the Lewis and Clark Expedition*. Glendale, CA: Arthur H. Clark, 1970. Contains biographical data on each member of the expedition, including the soldiers and boatmen who took the keelboat only as far as the Mandan villages and back to St. Louis. Interesting insights on the expedition, but somewhat dated.

Elliott Coues, ed., *The History of the Lewis and Clark Expedition*. 1893. Reprint, New York: Dover, 1982. Updated version of Nicholas Biddle's narrative, now published in three volumes. Includes much additional data not available to Biddle. Coues visited many of the sites.

Paul Russell Cutright, *A History of the Lewis and Clark Journals*. Norman: University of Oklahoma Press, 1976. The story of the publication of the Lewis and Clark journals is almost as exciting as the expedition itself. Biographies of the editors and publishers who made the journals available to the public. Later discoveries (diaries, notes, letters, etc.) are included.

———, *Lewis and Clark: Pioneering Naturalists*. Urbana: University of Illinois Press, 1969. Contains descriptions of plant and animal species observed and reported by Lewis and Clark. Many of these were unknown in the eastern part of the country at that time.

Dayton Duncan, *Out West: An American Journey*. New York: Viking Press, 1987. The author followed the Lewis and Clark Trail by automobile. Book includes many human-interest stories about people who live along the trail today.

John C. Ewers, *Indian Life on the Upper Missouri*. Norman: University of Oklahoma Press, 1968. Ethnographic accounts of the Sioux, Blackfeet, and other Upper Missouri Indian tribes. Discusses the changes that came about in those Indian nations after the Lewis and Clark expedition.

Patrick Gass, *A Journal of Voyages and Travels of a Corps of Discovery*. 1807. Reprint, with an introduction by Earle R. Forrest. Minneapolis: Ross and Haines, 1958. The diary of Patrick Gass, a sergeant on the Lewis and Clark expedition. The original diary has been lost, and the author's grammar, spelling, and writing style were greatly changed by the nineteenth-century publisher.

Jeff Hart, *Montana Native Plants and Early Peoples*. Helena: The Montana Historical Society, 1976. Illustrations and facts about wild plants used by Indians and settlers in Montana. Includes information on camas roots used as a food source by the Nez Percé, and by members of the expedition.

Donald Jackson, ed., *Letters of the Lewis and Clark Expedition*. Urbana: University of Illinois Press, 1978. Large collection of personal correspondence, official letters, and other documents related directly and indirectly to the expedition.

David Lavender, *The Way to the Western Sea: Lewis and Clark Across the Continent*. New York: Harper & Row, 1988. Highly readable narrative of the Lewis and Clark expedition based on the original journals but from a modern perspective. Contains interesting speculations about the motives of the principal characters.

Meriwether Lewis, *The Lewis and Clark Expedition*. 1814. Reprint, Philadelphia: J. B. Lippincott, 1961. After Lewis's death, Clark hired Nicholas Biddle to edit the journals of the expedition for publication. Biddle's work (on which his name did not appear) has become an American classic.

John C. Luttig, *Journal of a Fur-Trading Expedition on the Upper Missouri 1812–1813*. St. Louis: Missouri Historical Society, 1920. Luttig was a clerk at Fort Manuel, South Dakota. In this journal, he recorded the death of Charbonneau's wife at Fort Manuel in 1812. Most historians today believe he was referring to Sacagawea, the Shoshone woman on the Lewis and Clark expedition.

Gary E. Moulton, ed., *Atlas of the Lewis and Clark Expedition*. Lincoln: University of

Nebraska Press, 1983. Photographs of Captain Clark's maps of the expedition and his composite map of the West. Book includes an introduction by the editor.

————, *The Journals of the Lewis and Clark Expedition*. Lincoln: University of Nebraska, 1983. This multivolume edition of the original Lewis and Clark journals contains the most up-to-date information available about the expedition. More volumes are forthcoming.

Ernest Staples Osgood, *The Field Notes of Captain William Clark, 1803–1805*. New Haven, CT: Yale University Press, 1964. A packet of field notes kept by Captain Clark were found in an old house in St. Paul, Minnesota, in 1953. They were finally published after a long legal battle over ownership. Book contains photographs of the original notes.

Merrill D. Peterson, ed., *Thomas Jefferson: Writings*. New York: The Library of America, 1984. A collection of Thomas Jefferson's official letters and papers, his personal correspondence, and other writings.

Milo M. Quaife, ed., *The Journals of Captain Meriwether Lewis and Sergeant John Ordway*. Madison, WI: State Historical Society, 1916. Contains two journals discovered in 1913: a log kept by Lewis during his trip down the Ohio River and the lost journal of Sergeant Ordway. Both are published as originally written, with commentary by the editor.

James P. Ronda, *Lewis and Clark Among the Indians*. Lincoln: University of Nebraska Press, 1984. A skillful, sensitive analysis of the encounters Lewis and Clark had with Indian tribes. Contains valuable cultural information about the tribes before they were greatly changed.

M. O. Skarsten, *George Drouillard: Hunter and Interpreter for Lewis and Clark*. Glendale, CA: Arthur H. Clark, 1964. A tribute to the skillful frontiersman, hunter, and interpreter who performed outstanding service on the Lewis and Clark expedition.

Reuben Gold Thwaites, ed., *Original Journals of the Lewis and Clark Expedition, 1804-1806*. 1904-1905. Reprint, New York: Antiquarian Press, 1959. The complete journals were published for the first time to celebrate the hundredth anniversary of the Lewis and Clark expedition. Included in this modern eight-volume set are the diaries of Sergeant Floyd and Private Whitehouse, and the field maps of Captain Clark.

Olin D. Wheeler, *The Trail of Lewis and Clark, 1804–1904*. New York: G. P. Putnam's Sons, 1926. The author retraced the route of the Lewis and Clark expedition one hundred years afterward. Included in this two-volume set are Wheeler's diary and many photographs showing changes that had taken place during the century.

Index

Picture Credits

Cover Photo by Stock Montage

Yale Collection of Western Americana, Beinecke Rare Book and Manuscript Library, 23

The Bettmann Archive, 10, 17, 59, 75, 80, 87

Brown Brothers, 43, 79, 90

Culver Pictures, 12, 18, 28, 41, 53, 64, 97

Library of Congress, 11, 20, 95

Missouri Historical Society, 19, 22 (all), 27, 31, 68, 69, 72, 73, 92 (left)

National Museum of American Art, Washington, DC/Art Resource, NY, 33, 36, 38, 62, 85

North Wind Picture Archives, 15, 78

Oregon Historical Society, neg #38091, 34; neg # 4581, 50; neg # 4578, 77.

"Lewis and Clark at Three Forks" by E. S. Paxson, Courtesy of the Montana Historical Society, 57

Peabody Museum, Harvard University, Photograph by Hillel Burger, 45, 76

"Lewis and Clark Meeting Indians at Ross' Hole" by Charles M. Russell, Courtesy of the Montana Historical Society, 66

"York" by Charles M. Russell, Courtesy of the Montana Historical Society, Gift of the Artist, 39

Stock Montage, 46, 92 (right)

About the Author

Eleanor Hall is a freelance writer who has had several careers. For many years she taught sociology and anthropology at a community college in southern Illinois. After retiring from teaching, she became an educational counselor in an Illinois prison for a time. From 1988 to 1993, she worked as an interpreter of history, museum specialist, and writer for the National Park Service at the Gateway Arch in St. Louis.

While associated with the National Park Service, she wrote two curriculum guides, *The Oregon Trail: Yesterday and Today* and *When Two Worlds Met: An Observance of the Columbus Quincentennial.* For her curriculum guide on the Oregon Trail, she received the Midwest region's Tilden Award for outstanding performance in interpretation. She also is a contributor of feature articles to various periodicals.

Her interest in the Lewis and Clark expedition began while serving as an interpreter of history at the Museum of Westward Expansion at the Gateway Arch. She has visited many of the Lewis and Clark Trail sites discussed in this book.

She and her husband now live full-time in a travel trailer, moving seasonally wherever their interests take them.